B

y

KNOW LOVE

B
i
l
l

I
v
e
y

What is love - for?

Contact info for Bill Ivey: *KnowLove*TheBook@aol.com

Exhibits shown after the end of chapters are all either written by Bill Ivey, or otherwise owned by him, or are published herein with non-exclusive permission obtained from the authors or owners.

Special thanks:

To Judith Barban (author of Crown Jewels, Poplar River, Meredith's Wolf, et. al.) for early editing and literary consulting; to Brenda Wise and Francie Ivey for partial final editing; to Ray Pinkerton of Rehoboth Baptist Church for confirmation of consistency with God's Holy Word and Holy Spirit; to Francie for endless consulting, to Robyn Ivey and Jon-Michael Ivey for much needed computer consulting along the way, not to mention the exhibits that show their wonderfully inspired writing. Also, thanks to my sons Bill and Dallas Ivey, and so many other folks who had the patience to let me "bounce things off of them" to try to find the best answers to my *wonderings*. And of course special thanks to Mary Perdue, former First Lady of Georgia, Pierre Howard, former Lt Governor of Georgia, and Evangelist Gloria Gainor, for their beautiful endorsements of *Know Love*. Finally, thanks to my long time Bible Fellowship (Sunday School) teachers Ed Haley, Bill Cantrell, Charles Martin, and Frank Daniels, and the senior pastors at Rehoboth Baptist Church over the last thirty-something years. Without exception, each of the above persons named or otherwise referred to – each has been a special blessing for which I am eternally grateful.

Dedication with gratitude:

This book is dedicated to current and prospective little lambs and grown-up sheep, with gratitude to the One from whom all blessings flow.

Table of Contents

Biography   6
Seed for Thought   8

Chapter 1:   The Question   12
Chapter 2:   The Great Commission   19
Chapter 3:   Love is the Principal Principle   27

Chapter 4:   "But the Greatest of These Is…"   38
Chapter 5:   The Song Was Not About Me   55
Chapter 6:   But Why Is Life So Hard?   71

Chapter 7:   "Dem Bones Dem Bones Dem Dry Bones"   82
Chapter 8:   What It Was Was Football   90
Chapter 9:   Fearfully and Wonderfully Made   92

Chapter 10:   It's a Jungle Out There   140
Chapter 11:   Isaiah 43:7   147
Chapter 12:   The Classics   151

Chapter 13:   The Greatest Commandment   173
Chapter 14:   Conclusion from Know Love   179
Chapter 15:   Grace   187

Interlude: Shh – Prayer in Progress – In Love   194
              Intermission   206
              Shh – Prayer in Progress – In Love: continued – forever
                                                                        214

Chapter 16:   "T'was the Night *OF* Christmas"   252
Chapter 17:   Secret Things and A Merry Heart   260

In Memoriam   268

Chapter 18:   And That Is What Love Is - For   271

Epilogue: Where True Love Is, "*Sarah*" Will Be   278

Biography

Bill Ivey holds a BBA from Georgia State University and became the youngest CPA legally possible in the state of Georgia. He became the Controller of a multi-billion-dollar bank and bank holding company, Trust company of Georgia, predecessor of Sun Trust, as well as a partner in a CPA firm. He once walked from Nashville to Atlanta to be a speaker at and to encourage attendance at, the annual Pro-Life Rally at the Georgia State Capitol. In his fifties, he ran 91 miles in 24 hours to raise money for a Christian ministry. Among early distinctions, he served as co-captain of his high school football and track teams.

Ivey has published from a Christian viewpoint in newspapers and magazines across the state of Georgia for several decades. Know Love is his first book. He lives with his wife Francie and two of his four adult children in Tucker, Georgia, where for more than three decades he has been active in Rehoboth Baptist Church, a Southern Baptist Convention church.

At his church he has been a departmental director, a teacher, and a member of the church finance committee. For years he served as a chaplain to prison inmates through his father-in-law's ministry, Highways & Hedges Christian Ministries.

Born in LaGrange, Georgia, 1939, he was diagnosed with Leukemia in 2002. Now in 2016 he has a goal of living on earth longer than his parents (91 years each) and longer than his grandfather's 98 years. He even is wondering if we should seek to follow the example of Enoch, who "walked with God" and never died. He is trying to be keenly aware of opportunities for benefit from the long-life promise God offers in the Fifth Commandment for honoring your father and mother. God keeps His promises. So Ivey closes this biography by saying, with great appreciation, "It was such a blessing to be so loved by Daddy and Mother."

Seed for Thought

One Sunday morning at a small southern church, the new pastor called on one of his older deacons to lead in the opening prayer. The deacon stood up, bowed his head and said, "Lord, I hate buttermilk."

The pastor opened one eye and wondered where this was going. The deacon continued, "Lord, I hate lard." Now the pastor was totally perplexed. The deacon continued, "Lord, I ain't too crazy about plain flour. But after you mix 'em all together and bake 'em in a hot oven, I just love biscuits." He paused.

"Lord, help us to realize when life gets hard, when things come up that we don't like, whenever we don't understand what You are doing, that we need to wait and see what You are making. After You get through mixing and baking, it'll probably be something even better than biscuits. Amen."

(The above is with permission, from Mikey'sFunnies.com, hosted by Agathon Group, "website development and hosting with a ministry heart.")

I received the biscuit story from Robyn just barely in time to use it for this book opening. It fits. Now we *are* gonna bake batter for even better than biscuits. Better than biscuits? Like what? Love. We're gonna bake love.

Love is the most wonderful thing in the world. If you do not already know love, I suggest that you please let love capture your heart - and that you then watch as love continues to be the most important thing in your life throughout eternity.

Know Love gives guidance on how to be blessed and how to bless God. Think about it, from just a networking standpoint, wouldn't blessing Almighty God have the potential of being an infinitely valuable endeavor?

It is humbling and an honor and a privilege to even think about blessing God, and when you consider the benefits of doing so – infinitely valuable seems an accurate assessment.

*****

The greatest commandment is in Deuteronomy 6:5 and it says, "You shall love the Lord your God with all your heart, with all your soul, and with all your strength."

That would require quite a relationship, right?

How could you have such a relationship with anyone, much less God?

You can't see God like you can see other people, right?

You can't hear God like you can hear other people, right?

You can't hug God, right?

Then how in the world can you ever even come close to obeying the greatest commandment?

Who would command you to do the impossible?

So it must be possible. And even if you could not do it, just imagine the rewards from trying!

****

Remember Abraham, called the Father of Faith? He taught his unprecedented faith to Isaac. Then, just like Jesus had the power to avoid His crucifixion, bound, nailed to the cross, certainly Isaac, probably more than 20 years old, could have overpowered his probably more than 120 year-old father, rather than letting himself be bound on wood to be a burning sacrifice. Do you think Abraham was born with that kind of faith? Or do you think he set out on a grand journey to develop it? For any who do not know the story, at just the right time, God sent a lamb to die so Isaac could live.

Here's what I think about Abraham's faith. God "grew" that faith in Abraham. God allowed roadblocks and rewards in Abraham's paths that nurtured the faith. Abraham didn't have all that faith handed to him on a silver platter for the generations to come to marvel over. And just as God "grew" that faith in Abraham, He has set out to grow love in you and me.

Now, before we set out to "*Know Love*," let's consider what we know so far. Frequently the question "Why" is important. "Why" did God create you? My little brother, shortly before he passed away, said

potential is, "Being used for that purpose for which you were created."

So, on a micro scale, "Why did God create you?"

Chapter 1:
The Question

Francie and I have been married more than three decades. It all began six days before Christmas, 1981. The party was at the house of my brother, Bob, and his wife, Melnee. Francie is Melnee's sister. Actually it was a birthday party, Jesus' of course, but December 19 was the birthday of Scott (Bob and Melnee's third child) and it was also Francie's birthday. A "fine" coincidence, as Andy Taylor might say.

When I overheard Francie tell someone, "My car wouldn't start, but a friend offered me a ride, so I came on anyway, with the faith that someone would give me a ride home," I knew that *someone* was going to be me. It was just a matter of how would I let *her* know that. She was at one end of the buffet table, I was at the other. I needed to move fast, and not lose my chance. I was so cool as I all of a sudden wanted only the food near her.

Francie and Melnee were two of six children in their family, and I only remember having seen Francie on one other occasion. And nothing clicked then. But now Francie had a magnetic attraction that commanded my attention. And I grew to love her over time. It is the same way with God. When we come to understand God is attractive, because He is good and perfect in every possible way, and we come to know He loves us, do we automatically love Him? Not exactly the same, but yes definitely. At first we don't even grasp that He is good and perfect in every possible way. And we certainly can't grasp the immeasurable depth of His love for us. But we learn of our need for Him. Then it is as we come to know Him that we grow to love Him.

I could see Francie with my eyes. No one has ever seen God with their eyes. Yes, Jesus said He and His Father are One. But I haven't seen Jesus with my eyes either, right? So how can I grow to love Him?

Bonding may be how spirit grows to love Spirit - the bonding of our heart, soul, strength, might, mind - it is through God's knitting together of the entire soul that we learn to love. And therein lies the greatest commandment - but let's not go there yet. For now, let's just begin with what God did first, and why. Psalm 139:13-14 ESV says, "...you knitted me together in my mother's womb. I praise you, for I am fearfully and wonderfully made..."

But why? "Why did God create us, anyway?" Those are the words I heard a distraught woman muttering as I was going to the greeting card section of a drug store and she was leaving. She seemed very distressed. So why did He create us? How did such a thought occur to Him?

"Did it ever occur to you that nothing ever occurred to God?"

That was the title of a message delivered by Bobby Smith at Rehoboth Baptist Church in Tucker, Georgia many years ago. God can see everything in the future more clearly than we can see anything in the present. Therefore, everything that has happened so far did not include anything that surprised God. When He created Adam and Eve, He already knew they would sin, and that He would send Jesus to pay the horrible price for their sin. Adam and Eve were created perfect. And they were created with a free will.

But why? Why did God do all that? One purpose of this writing is to suggest a missing link, the answer to that question, the question most asked by children, "Why?," and the question frequently asked by inquisitive adults at their wit's end, "Why did God create us?" I sought the answer from my wife, Francie, whom God had given me by not blessing her with a more dependable car. She then gave me this journal entry she had written in 1971, while she was a student at Tennessee Temple University.

> Everything
> Is too wide.
> Too all inclusive,
> Too enveloping,
> And too profound
> For anyone to possibly learn it all,
> Or even to completely comprehend
> One minute part of its infinity;

Because of its dependencies
And interrelations.

If one
Starts at one point
And tries to proceed
Logically from there,
He only ends up frustrated
Because he has
Inevitably digressed
From his course.

Time,
Ability,
And memory lapses
Are barriers
Preventing the completion
Of a line of thought.
How can anyone completely master
Any phase of everything
Without mastering everything itself?

Dependencies,
Affinities,
Associations
And relevancies
Are all tangible,
And divert one's attention from
Any certain mental pathway.

They repress minds
From continuing
The search for
The knowledge
Of everything
And anything.

Bewilderment,
Disillusionment,
And feelings of futility

Discourage attempts
To attain wisdom.

Only God knows everything.
Only God can reveal—
Or retain
Everything
Or anything
To everyone—
Or anyone.

He locks and opens our minds.
He will let us
Know—
In His own time.
We must pray for
The right knowledge
At the right time.

That didn't answer my question. So I ignored the fact that her journal entry looked like a poem but didn't even rhyme, and decided to go with the part about, "Only God knows everything. Only God can reveal - - ." But first I pressed Francie further. I insisted that if Francie knew the answer to this crucially important question that she give it to me. Now!

She just smiled and gave me this poem she wrote in the 5th grade:

I have the answer
    that you need
Some words of wisdom
    you should heed
That if you knew
    might help a lot
I'd tell you – only -
    I forgot!

Well at least that poem rhymed, but where could there be found the answer to so profound a question? People everywhere would love to know.

Since I had learned to this point, "Only God knows everything, only God can reveal," my search took me first to the Bible and, eventually, to God Himself.

"The Question"
-poem by Bill and Francie's daughter Robyn Ivey

IF ONLY
I KNEW JUST WHAT
TO SAY, MY   WRITER'S BLOCK
WOULD GO   AWAY. I'D LOSE
THE STATIC   IN MY MIND, AND
ELOQUENTLY   I WOULD FIND
THE WORDS   TO TELL YOU
WHAT IS REAL   AND LET YOU
KNOW JUST   HOW I FEEL.
EMOTIONS
CHANGE AND
SO DO I, LIKE
OCEAN WAVES
AS TIME GOES BY.
THIS CONSTANT
CHANGE CONFUSES
ME, BUT NOT FOR
L O N G, PARCE QUE
"C'EST LA VIE!"
AN IDEA COMES
INTO MY BRAIN.
THIS FLEETING
THOUGHT DOES
NOT REMAIN.
I'M LIMITED
BY TIME AND
SPACE, AND
WHEN I THINK I
LOSE MY PLACE.

THE HUMAN
BRAIN IS QUITE
COMPLEX. I NEVER
KNOW WHAT'S
COMING NEXT.
DO YOU?

Chapter 2
The Great Commission

"Let me show you pictures of my grandchildren." I have said that

a few times. But what I would rather do now is show my grandchildren

the story of my baby brother. I am sure I had plenty of joy before my

earliest recollection of it, but my earliest recollection of joy was the day

Bob became ten months old. He was seven years younger than me. He

took ten steps on that day. I know, that is not a monumental

accomplishment, but I remember the joy that I had. Nine steps would not

have been significant, nor would eleven. But ten on his ten month

birthday. I was so excited.

Yes, that was the excitement of a little boy, and I was part of a

cheering section on the front porch of the house on the corner, on Johnson

Street, in Hogansville, Georgia. And he was happy about it all too. But

the coincidence of ten on ten, it all seemed so marvelous to me. The Lord

had planted a seed.

Today I just realized, that joy was the joy of the Lord. It was some

months after I accepted the Lord as my savior that I realized that

coincidences happened all over the place and they weren't coincidences.

And I began to love "coincidences." I mean that first recollection was

really no big deal. But as I look back, the joy I felt was similar to the joy I feel when I see the Lord in little things, and the frequency of the happenings just blows me away since I know, as a numbers person, that so many such happenings statistically are so unlikely to occur by chance that it is a certainty to me that the Lord is in it, and saying, "Hi there, just letting you know I'm still with you, and I love you."

But this chapter is first of all to tell my grandchildren about their great-uncle Bob. And maybe even more importantly, it is to tell Bob's grandchildren, whom he never met, about their wonderful granddaddy. So I will proceed.

First though, one more coincidence. I can't resist. Most of the coincidences are little things, each of which would take prohibitively long to tell about, and it is their frequency in unlikely circumstances that makes them remarkable. This one is bigger, and standing alone does not seem a gigantic coincidence. It is the smaller but high frequency of coincidences that clinches that they are not coincidences. But I love this one. On the Decatur High School football team, Bob was one of only two players who were starters as a sophomore, and later they were elected co-captains as seniors. He was also co-captain of the track team. Well, seven years earlier, his big brother, whom he loved, also was one of only two players who were starters as a sophomore, and they (also) were elected co-captains as seniors. He was (also) co-captain of the track team.

Some of many other things I consider interesting about Bob were, he was co-president of the student body at Decatur, and his senior year he was chosen by The Atlanta Journal as the lineman of the year for Greater Atlanta. At Vanderbilt, for his total senior year, he was the SEC's number one tight end in pass receiving yardage. And he caught a diving, horizontal, catch for a touchdown (to tie Navy 35-35) that the Nashville Banner veteran sports writer called, "... arguably the greatest catch in Vanderbilt history." Later, he and Melnee were house parents for a house of children at Baptist Children's Home in Nashville for several years.

I guess I should tell you this part too, since it relates to him, and coincidences, and this coincidence seemed important from the beginning. In 1988 Bob was suffering from ALS, Lou Gehrig's Disease, a disease in which the muscles become less and less able, and eventually the body ceases to function. I came to believe that God wanted me to fast for forty days, on Bob's behalf. I didn't really think I could. The first two days seemed surprisingly easy. I still didn't think there was much chance I would really fast for forty days.

After the first two days though, I decided to look at the calendar and see what day would be the last day of the forty days, just in case this was for real. I couldn't believe what I saw. *The fortieth day would be Bob's birthday.* I was shocked and scared. I recounted and recounted. How could this be? I chose to not even drink water for the next three days, this was obviously important, and I didn't want to risk doing anything wrong.

Bob passed away on 7-11-88, and I completed the forty days successfully on 8-5-88, Bob's 42nd birthday. *I was further blown away when I later learned 8-5-88 was also the 134th "birthday" of my church, Rehoboth Baptist Church in Tucker.*

So what was the point of the forty-day fast, and it ending on Bob's and my church's birthday? I still don't have an answer, but "…we know that all things work together for good to those who love God, to those who are the called according to His purpose" (Romans 8:28). Perhaps it was just one step in preparing me to write this book. As one pastor said, "God is preparing you today for what He has for you tomorrow."

Bob spent a large part of his last year going around to groups like the Fellowship of Christian Athletes, and speaking to the groups from his wheelchair, and passing the message to "find a flock to feed." That's part of the Great Commission, to go into all the world, teaching all things whatsoever that Jesus taught us. I think 'whatsoever' even includes things disguised as coincidences. And writing is one excellent way to fulfill the Great Commission.

Bob was the *funnest* guy you could ever meet. Everybody loved him. He was a great speaker. He became the marketing director for a publicly traded corporation. And after he passed away they dedicated their next annual report to stockholders to him. And they established a scholarship fund in his memory at Decatur High School. Why? Because they loved him. Thank you, Mr. Jerry Eickhoff, for making it happen.

TWO EXHIBITS WRITTEN BY MY LITTLE BROTHER:

This is My Life

by Bob Ivey,
September 10, 1958

12 years 1 month 2 days 23 hours and 1 minute from the time I am writing this, my mother had triplets, me, myself, and I. We all had a good time together and were very close.

That was after the war when my father was a captain in the 21st Engineers. After the war, he worked as a Purchasing Agent at U. S. Rubber Company. We then lived in Hogansville, where Daddy was elected a City Councilman and elected President of the Kiwanis Club. It was here that my brother made the immortal statement, "If you keep moving up you'll be eligible for the Lions Club."

Later we moved to Thomson where he worked for Knox Homes and now he is here working for Rich's.

Oh, by the way, he was second in his high school graduating class. (There weren't but two people.)

In my mother's schooling, she was voted prettiest and ugliest girl of the school. There was one group that was mad at her and another who liked her.

I've got a sister and brother, both older, you might say I'm the baby of the family.
My brother and I are different from most brothers, we get along fine together.
My sister is married with a twenty month old baby boy, and expecting a new arrival in October.

Every summer I visit her house for a couple of weeks, and this summer was no exception. I went horse-back riding, and water skiing but the most fun was taking care of the baby.

My favorite sport is football and my favorite college team is Auburn, first in the SouthEastern conference, and in the nation last year.

Next comes baseball, my favorite team in that is Las Angeles, but my encouragement doesn't seem to help, with luck they'll end up in seventh place.

If Winnona doesn't come in first place in football my name isn't Dan McKinney.

For awhile chemistry was a hobby with me, but while I was making an experiment the bottle blew up in my face, so now I collect stamps.

One of the things I have enjoyed most has been going to my grandmother's house with my brother, and bringing back my grandmother.

She lives in Grove Hill Alabama, about 300 miles away. She is the best grandmother anyone ever had.

My whole family is a good one, and the best family I ever had.

A Shepherd in Sheep's Clothing:

Why can't I walk, God? And why can't I play?
And wrestle the kids at the end of each day?

Why can't it be like it always was before?
Why can't I play tennis, or run anymore?

I don't understand, God, And the price is too steep.
Then the echo came back:
Just go feed my sheep.

Easy for you, you're a shepherd by trade
A rod and a staff, and you've got it made...

You seem to forget, that I was also a sheep.
A sacrificed Lamb; the cross, too, is steep.

And all that I ask for your role to be
Is that when people see you, they also see me.

Because, Bob, we're together while climbing this hill;
We're living each day, seeking God's will.

A miracle is happening, and Joy follows sorrow.
But we need a perfect vantage point from which to view tomorrow.

Your weakness makes me stronger, And my strength is all we need.
By my stripes you're healed already, So let's find a flock to feed.

Bob Ivey, ALS Patient

August 5, 1946 – July 11, 1988

Chapter 3:
Love is the Principal Principle

The Bible says David was a man after God's own heart. Why would David be so special to God? I mean David had multiple wives and concubines. David even sent a man into battle to be killed, just so he could take the man's wife. God disciplined him for that, but why would David rank so highly with righteous Almighty God?

Yes, David was in line to be blessed because of God's covenant with his ancestor, Abraham. Abraham was so faithful to God that God promised that Abraham's descendants would possess his land forever (Genesis 13:14-17). And truly God had already blessed Abraham's descendant, David, before David's shortcomings came to light. But although God looks on the heart, God also sees the future, and He knew exactly what David's behavior was going to be before He blessed David. Still, God really appreciated David. Why?

The key is David acknowledged God lovingly more frequently than just about anybody, and with enormous passion. He delighted in God. He spent time with God. When God pointed out his mistakes, he humbly agreed with God, and changed directions. David courted God's favor. He sang God's praises. If you court someone, it means you give them your special attention. If you court someone with passionate love, it means even more to them. Obviously, God appreciated that. David was a living profile showing Love Is the Principal Principle.

However, the Biblical statement that David was a man after God's own heart literally speaks of David's motive, not God's response. It doesn't tell us that God loved David more than God loved Abraham or Joseph, or you or me, or a terrorist. It does though, imply God highly favors the positive actions of David, it suggests that God delighted in those actions. God could NOT love David more than the 100% unconditional love He has for you and me. As a partner in a CPA firm, I'm telling you 100% is all there is. And 100% unconditional love from God is enough for anybody. Nothing you can ever do will make God love you more (or less) than He does right now. But the question at hand is, "Why 'in the world' did God create us?"

Genesis 1:27 says, "So God created man in His own image, in the image of God He created him; male and female He created them". Why? Why did He do that?

Love. "But what about what it says in Isaiah 43...."

I know. But just be *patient*, love. We'll get to that. 'Love' is not self-seeking, and does not want to distract from God's 'glory', but maybe it is time to give credit where credit is due. God created us because of love.

And it's a good thing love is patient (I Cor. 13:4). Why? Because God gave Adam just one simple rule and he broke it. Then God gave us the Ten Commandments. We broke every single one of them, over and over again. Then, first through Moses and then through Jesus, God told us the greatest commandment is to Love.

It's like starting with Rules-Based Accounting, and then being told about Principles- Based Accounting. You still need to reference the rules after you learn the principles, but the principles are the alpha and the omega, the goal, the facilitator, the ideal, and the joy that results in a beauty to behold.

It was August 20, 2009. My recently departed mother would have been ninety-four years old that day. I was at an accounting seminar. It was very boring, until the speaker began discussing Principles Based Accounting versus Rules Based Accounting. I didn't even know what that meant. The Biblical parallel seemed striking. And my mind stayed focused on that.

For several days, a song had been going through my head. The words repeatedly were, "I been cheated, been mistreated, when will I be loved?" It wasn't true. Not for me. I am very loved. Maybe I just liked the tune. I don't remember any more of the words, but I really do like the tune. It ran through my head in class, and I began thinking about love. Everybody in the world is loved. Everybody.

Okay back to the class. I "think" Principles Based Accounting (like the principle of love) is necessary in order for the world to be able to trust the financial statements produced by companies. Without principles, rules are of no worthwhile value. Without principles, rules are of no worthwhile value, but children need to follow the rules before they are advanced enough to grasp the principles.

Rules Based Accounting (think of the Ten Commandments and other Biblical admonitions) is necessary in order to help people focus and apply the accounting principles (think of faith, hope and love).

Example: The number one principle of God is love. But it is a long-term principle (eternal) in its perspective. So like children, we experience for our own good what does not immediately seem like love, and we are guided toward being better-developed persons. In growing us, God has taken into account everything that will ever happen as a result of His and our actions (Romans 8:28).

Example continued: God gave the commandment, "Thou shalt not kill" to help people interpret and apply the principle of love. But the principle (love) is primary, and the rule ("Thou shalt not kill") is a helper.

"Thou shalt not kill" is a rule. But God also gave us a brain. If a deadly snake is about to strike a helpless baby, would God have us interpret His rule as saying, "Thou shalt not kill the snake", and thereby let the baby die? The answer to the contrary is obvious, because *the purpose of the rule is to guide us to use the principle, yet the principle of love "rules over" any rule.*

You kill the venomous snake, following and experiencing the principle of love, and you save the loved and innocent baby. That may seem like a 'no-brainer', but properly balancing any principle and its related rules really does require a brain. Frequently, it requires a brain that has an open mind as to our actions, but still a mind first and foremost tuned in 100% to God's Holy Word and its principles and rules, with the comforting help of the Holy Spirit.

Love is the principal principle. That is why it stands as the verb in the greatest commandment. In Matthew 22, paraphrasing, Jesus said we should love God with all our everything, and secondly, we should love other people as we love ourselves.

1 John 4:8 says, "…God is love". Acting unrighteously evidences a deficiency of love. God has no deficiency. God is 100% Love. And He also is 100% righteous. He grasps that unrighteousness hurts someone somewhere, sometime, and Love is not willing to hurt someone, unless, like with the snake, it is expression of greater love. As a wise Father, He allows us to learn about love/righteousness from our mistakes, i.e. the hard way, if we insist. And our nature is to insist.

Though Jesus died for our sins, like a big brother willing to take a beating to rescue a guilty little brother, but on a more dramatic and eternal scale, Jesus never committed one sin. Not one. God is love, and Jesus as part of the Holy Trinity is God, and since acting unrighteously evidences a deficiency of love, and Love cannot have a deficiency of itself, Jesus never did anything wrong. Eventually the only way to avoid doing wrong is to BE love. God knows that. And that is why Jesus said to Love God with everything we've got, because it puts us in a right relationship with God/Love (100% Love) and the result - it is good. Think of it this way. God is pure love. If we can love Him with pure love, it is His love flowing through us, to Him, and nothing could be more pure nor more desirable, completely without fault, and full of grace and truth, giving unselfishly with honor, to the one deserving of all honor and all glory and all praise.

In accounting, debits must equal credits. Apparently that is also a spiritual requirement. If God could give everybody a free ride to heaven without them believing on Jesus and being appreciative of what He did for us, maybe He would. Maybe Love would, so maybe He would. But evil exists. God didn't create evil and heaven wouldn't be heaven if evil were there, and it never will be there. Hell was created for Satan and all who choose to follow Him there. I don't understand why it has to be that way (Prov. 3:5). But actions have consequences, so those who refuse to exercise their free will to be on God's side, His omniscient way, will follow Satan to his eventual destination. When Adam disobeyed God and ate from the tree of the knowledge of good and evil, a process began. And while the Good News is that God gave Jesus to rescue us from what we deserve from that process, if we will not to accept Jesus, thereby rejecting God's precious, very, very expensive, perfect gift, it leaves the only other alternative for us. Eventually the books WILL be balanced.

If God is love, and He is, and if Satan is evil, and he is, then when you love someone, it is God loving through you. If you hate someone, it is Satan hating through you. Your part is to allow it or not. Love does not hate people. Love (the verb) does passively hate evil. Love loves love, and hating evil is an inactive byproduct from love of the love that love loves. To actively hate is to kill spiritually, and Love will kill the snake not out of hate but because love loves the helpless baby that evil despises.

Someone said, "What we do for God may be important. What we let God do through us is eternally important." Who said that? Me, I think. Or God through me?

In Bible Fellowship Class, my teacher, Frank Daniels, said, "I think sometimes God delights in us!" I think Frank was right. A loving Father often delights in his children. Bob Warren, of the Fellowship of Christian Athletes, wrote, "Allow the joy that you bring the Lord through your obedience to be the motivating factor in your life."

Wow, what a reason to be obedient. To bring joy to the Lord. WE can do that.

But Jesus said the greatest commandment is to love God with all our heart, all our soul, all our strength, all our might, all our mind, all our everything. Are we that obedient? You can't run a marathon or even a great one hundred meter dash the first day you start training.

You might want to start with the last four words in Psalms. "Praise ye the Lord!"

That is a rule like in Rules Based Accounting. But what a wonderful example of a rule that is so important in moving toward what Jesus referred to as the greatest commandment. When we move closer with that rule, moving closer to the greatest commandment, we can truly see, Love is the Principal Principle.

I recently read that children spell "love" t-i-m-e. They assume the amount of time you spend with them shows how much you love them. God is willing to give us as much of His time as we want.

You have God's love whether you obey Him or not. Just as my children have mine. But if you want His favor, you need to give Him some of your time. If you love Him enough to want to give him joy, enough to want to cause Him to delight in you, rejoice in Him and delight in Him, as you trust His omniscience and His love, in sweet obedience to Him.

Is it possible to love God with all your heart, all your soul, all your strength, all your might, all your mind, which Jesus said is the greatest commandment? Years before my mother passed away, she teasingly asked my three-year-old daughter if my daughter loved her a 'litta bit'. Robyn picked up on the tease and replied, "No, I don't." Then with joy in her voice she came back with, "I love you a lotta bit!" That became a humorous bond between them, which they returned to very often. Make a conscious effort to really really love God, even if it starts out being just a litta bit, and you just might find that you soon move toward loving Him with the kind of passion He loves you. And that's more than even ... a lotta bit.

The words on the next page reflect "The Love Chapter" of the Bible. Nothing could be easier to love than Love.

*****

Special note of gratitude: The plaque that follows was a wedding present given to Francie and me by John Cross and his wife. John Cross was the Gideon who led me to the Lord.

Chapter 4:

"But the Greatest of These Is…"

The way we act sometimes, you would think 1 Corinthians 13:13 says, "…faith, hope and fear, these three; but the greatest of these is fear." No way! It says, "And now abide faith, hope, love, these three; but the greatest of these *is* love".

2 Timothy 1:7 says, "For God has not given us a spirit of fear, but of power and of love and of a sound mind". So why do we abide fear with our faith and hope? I think it is because when we are challenged by fear, we naturally fall back on our faith and our hope *defensively*. We forget all about love. Our team has Love. In football vernacular, Love is the greatest offense the world has ever known, and we forget and start only playing *defense*. We let the fear cast out love. That is exactly what fear wants to do. It wants us to think *defensively* of *ourselves*, use our faith and our hope defensively, and fear for *ourselves*.

That's just backwards! We shouldn't focus on the potentially approaching storm, rather than Jesus - and His love - and all He has done for us, *and all He wants to do for us*. Love is the principal principle, so why would we want to forget all about love, just when we need it most?

I John 4:18, 19 says, "There is no fear in love; but perfect love casts out fear, because fear involves torment. But he who fears has not been made perfect in love. We love Him because He first loved us".

I have to admit, in my adult life, many times I have messed up and fear has gotten the best of me and left me and my loved ones with the worst of me. And yes, the presence of fear is very destructive. And we all need help sometimes.

When faced with fear, faith and hope are good. But why forget about God's *best*? Love. "…all things work together for good to those who love the Lord and are the called according to His purpose" (Romans 8:28). And, paraphrasing John 3:16, God so loves *you*!

If you have accepted Jesus as your Savior, savor the fact that the Holy Spirit now abides in you. When we let fear torment us, we are letting forgetfulness take away our primary spiritual weapon. Love. Love is the stuff courage is made of. It really is. God loves us, He is Omniscient, He is Omnipotent, the Holy Spirit is with us to comfort us, and "Love never fails…" (1 Corinthians 13:8). And remember, those words exact are on the plaque. Love never fails.

Think on this. Love and fear are decisions that we make with our free will, sometimes conscious decisions, but more often, we make these decisions without considering that we are making decisions. Yet we exactly are doing that. Maybe it is not your fault if a bird lands on your head, but you can keep it from building a nest there. Fear can come on a person quickly, but it should be dealt with before it becomes a big problem, and the way to do that is through God's Love and His Power.

Surprisingly, we can't choose both love and fear. These are two purposeful opposing weapons of spiritual warfare. Sure, we try hard to not be afraid. Nobody likes to be afraid. But are we knowledgeable enough to know what to do when a spirit of fear arrives? How 'in the world' are we humans supposed to deal with something like 'spiritual warfare'? What's that all about? Romans 8: 6 says, "For to be carnally minded is death; but to be spiritually minded is life and peace." Unsurprisingly, our soul cannot be primarily in a state of both carnal mindedness and spiritual mindedness at the same time.

What do bullies feed on? The victim's fear. If you are not afraid of them, if you have a big brother who can clean their clock, and you are always singing your big brother's praises, what does it remind the bullies of?

Obviously they can't feed on your fear when you are simply excited that your big brother is going to use them to mop the floor for you. In this example, Jesus is the big brother. Satan is the bully. I'm not taunting, just stating a fact. When we are weak, He is Strong.

> James 4: 7, 8 says, "Submit yourselves therefore to God. Resist the devil, and he will flee from you. Draw nigh to God, and He will draw nigh to you."

Resist him...and he will flee.
Draw near to Him...and He will draw near to you.

When I was a small boy, on Halloween, I became separated from my big sister somehow, and I was walking from the porch of a dark house, nobody was home, and the street in small town Hogansville, Georgia, seemed so very, very dark. I was all alone. I started repeating the twenty-third Psalm. In retrospect, I think I 'got dumber' as I grew up. Quoting God's Word to Him is an excellent way to get His attention, His appreciation, and His help, and a great way to get yourself some comfort and renewed strength in the face of the unknown, and the unknown is exactly what a spirit of fear attacks us with. And quoting God's Word to Him is a great way to let perfect love cast out a spirit of fear and allow you to reclaim a spirit of power and of love and of a sound mind. Somehow, that small boy did seem to know, really, we never are alone. Jesus said, "I will never leave you nor forsake you" (Hebrews 13:5).

To paraphrase Frank Daniels in Bible Fellowship at Rehoboth Baptist Church in Tucker, GA, 10-18-09:

Fear is a normal, necessary defensive reaction to danger. But when you are afraid,

    1. Admit your fear.

    2. Focus on God. (And Frank would concur, while focusing on God remember 1 John 4:8, "…God is love.")

    3. Follow through with praise.

Did David have fear, and did he praise God? Oh, did he ever!

Check out Psalm 56: 3-4 KJV:

> What time I am afraid, I will trust in thee. In God I will praise his word, in God I have put my trust; I will not fear what flesh can do unto me.

And the same Psalm in the New King James translation:

> Whenever I am afraid, I will trust in You. In God (I will praise His word), In God I have put my trust; I will not fear. What can flesh do to me?

Now read Psalm 56: 9-13:

> When I cry out *to You,*
> Then my enemies will turn back;
> This I know, because God *is* for me.
> In God (I will praise *His* word),
> In the LORD (I will praise *His* word),
> In God I have put my trust;
> I will not be afraid.
> What can man do to me?

Finally, the Psalmist continues the last two of these verses expressing commitment and praise in appreciative thankfulness, all now evidencing his power in God:

> Vows made to You are binding upon me, O God;

I will render praises to You,
For You have delivered my soul from death.
Have You not kept my feet from falling,
That I may walk before God
In the light of the living?

Praise in truth was how David overcame fear, combining that with a renewal of vows of devotion to God. This obligation to give praise and thanksgiving was actually a joy to David.

Here is a possibility to let love cast out fear: Psalm 37:4 says, "Delight yourself also in the LORD, And He shall give you the desires of your heart."

Does your heart really want to get rid of fear? How do you accomplish delighting yourself in the Lord? Spend time with Him (Bible and conversation, which includes listening) and ask Him to help you delight in Him. He has all the time in the world, and He would be delighted to help you delight in Him. He delights in your obedience as He guides you into the most prosperous paths for your soul, because He loves you. And when sometimes it seems He is not listening, keep on keeping on, because whenever it most seems you have been backed up against a wall, that is precisely when God has the most good things in process for you. Jesus would always take in His arms the little lamb that needed

Him. Isaiah 26:3 declares to God, "You will keep him in perfect peace whose mind is stayed on You. Because he trusts in You." (Amen.)

If you really want to delight yourself in Him, start looking for the little things that He is doing. He is always doing. And He is always doing for you. "You can see a lot just by looking!" - said Yogi Berra, though not nearly on this subject. (Consider these notes I made from the May 2008 issue of the *Ladies Home Journal* " Five Habits of Happy People.": Make a point of noticing everything good that happens to you, any positive thought you have, about anything you see, feel, taste, hear or smell, or otherwise experience, that brings you honorable pleasure. This intention to notice activates the reticular activating system, *RAS*, a group of cells at the base of the brain stem. Once you notice something positive, take time to savor it to habitually feed happiness - and it will grow. That's right, feed happiness and it will grow.)

I have found encouraging results by following the above notes, and adding another wrinkle, again borrowing from the Yogi Berra hint. Feeling down? Ask God for encouragement. Then look for it, and it will come. It may come in an unexpected way, or with seeming delay, but look for it and it will come.

God is a positive God, and I positively believe that the reticular activating system at the base of the brain stem was not put there by accident. Throughout the Bible God encourages thankfulness and praise, and the RAS - well, just practice telling God, "Thank You," and praise Him whenever you can find the smallest reason to be happy, then see if you can be - as happy as you can be. And you know what they say, "Practice makes perfect." Reflect on what the prophet Isaiah wrote:

> You will keep him in perfect peace,
> Whose mind is stayed on You,
> Because he trusts in You (Isaiah 26:3).

Everyone should memorize that verse. Write it down, and tape it to your desk or wherever you will see it every day. One day it could save the day for you.

Sarah Young's book, *Jesus Calling*, said that there is one problem with the picture we have of the future. It is a false picture. It is a false picture because as we are visualizing a difficulty, Jesus is not in the picture, and He has promised, "I will never leave you nor forsake you." So someone has tricked us into buying into a false picture. Hey, Jesus was even in the fiery furnace with Shadrach, Meshach and Abednego. And that is why they lived to tell the tale.

God could have kept Shadrach, Meshach and Abednego from being thrown into the fiery furnace. But instead, God received great glory and taught a spiritual principle we can learn from today. He let that happen, letting them then be seen in the fiery furnace, with Him, and they did not even get singed - or even sweat in the fire. Don't sweat the future. God is in control. Abide with Him, and enjoy the fun.

Now, I try to remember whenever I look at a picture of the future, to try to truthfully visualize the Lord with me in the picture. I don't see any fear when the Lord is with me, as He is right now. And the future? I have His Word on it.

What about fear right now? In Linda Sommer's book *You Can Take It With You,* "A Daily Devotional Guide For Doing God's Word," she says, "Fear blocks awareness of God's presence." We should always be focusing on an awareness of God's presence. That should be a byproduct of complying with Jesus' revelation that men ought always to pray. It is clear that a spirit of a tormenting fear is a companion of Satan. And his fear will flee with him when you resist him (James 4:7), by properly focusing on that awareness of God's presence.

One of my favorite stories regarding fear is in Luke 2:10, 11 KJV, where the angel of the Lord says, at the first Christmas, "Fear not: for, behold, I bring you good tidings of great joy, which shall be to all people. For unto you is born this day in the city of David a Savior, which is Christ the Lord." God knows we are subject to fear, so He starts with words of reassurance. And we've still got those good tidings of great joy. They are ours to keep. And we are His great joy! Why? Because He loves us.

Starting with the fact God loves you so, so much, notice the happy things in your life, no matter how small, thereby activating that reticular activating system (RAS). In Psalm 139:14, the psalmist says, "I will praise You, for I am fearfully and wonderfully made. Marvelous are Your works..." When God made you, He knew exactly what He was doing. Exactly. Proverbs 17:22 says, "A merry heart does good, like medicine,..." So give it a try. Go to the inter net and follow the Bobby McFerrin song, "Don't Worry Be Happy".

In summary, after thousands of years of quiet proclamation from Proverbs 17:22, it seems medical science and the musical world concur, "A merry heart does good, like medicine."

And oh, like Columbo would say, there's one more thing. Although the Manufacturer's Warranty specifies in John 3:16 only one requirement for full redemption, the Owner's Manual is filled with specifications for optimal operating results. The older the vehicle, the more need seems to arise to address difficulties, as bumpy roads of life and abuse of instructions takes a toll. The single greatest instruction for operating results is found in at least four places in the Owner's Operating Manual: Deuteronomy 6:5, Matthew 22:37, Mark 12:30, and Luke 10:27. Same instruction, from four different places, and the Manufacturer guarantees it is the greatest instruction.

Finally, the Owner's Manual specifies 365 times "fear not." Over and over again it says, "Rejoice!" It even says, "Let everything that has breath praise the Lord. Praise ye the Lord!" But why do so few people know what the Manufacturer calls the greatest instruction? Please pay very close attention here. The Manufacturer says the greatest instruction is "Thou shalt love the Lord thy God with all thy heart, and with all thy soul, and with all thy strength, and with all thy mind..." But people don't talk about that. Why not?

For best operating results, follow the Manufacturer's instructions, and love God with everything you've got. "And now abide faith, hope, love, these three; but the greatest of these *is* love."

*****

Jane's Soccer Game:

She was a beautiful baby. Dallas, my second son, and Teilynn, his wife, did not know that until after they had flown to the hotel in Fuzhou City, Fujian Province, China, to meet Jane; and the orphanage, several hours away but still in Fujian Province, brought Jane to them for the meeting. *But it was a sort of made in Heaven kind of* **love** *before first sight.* They didn't tell me that. But 1 John 4:8 says, "God is love." And you don't fly thousands of miles to adopt someone you have never seen for just no reason. And I say, "The reason was Love"

And now Jane was a beautiful little girl in Tucker, Georgia. It was a few years later at her soccer game at Henderson Park. Dallas was one of two coaches for her team, but he was away at an annual golfing retreat. He only plays golf once a year, and this was the once for the year.

I was early for Jane's soccer game, and sitting there thinking about the chapter I had written on "fear." I was thinking again about 2 Timothy 1:7 saying, "For God has not given us a spirit of fear, but of power and of love and of a sound mind." And I noticed for the first time that it was not talking about regular fear, it was talking about a whole *spirit* of fear. And that made sense. Fear is one thing - if it is just something to consider, decide about, and move on - but a *spirit* of fear was something entirely different. A spirit of fear could be a spirit that would linger, after a problem, and nag, and pester, and fester, and be ready to jump on just about any new thought with complete negativity. I decided I needed to get this view into the book. But then I figured, "No, I won't remember it, I will think about dozens of other things before I get home to write it down, and I won't remember it at all."

But exactly then, something happened that changed my mind.

Jane's coach came walking across the small soccer field toward the man sitting next to me, and as soon as he was in hearing distance, still coming, he called out, "This is so weird. I wrote down all the names of the girls on the team, in random order, and have been checking them off as they arrived, and that is the sequence in which they have been arriving! Every one of them. There are just two more, Susan and Mary - oh, and there is Susan's dad...and there comes Susan behind him...oh and there comes Mary - wrote down all the names in random order and that is the exact order that every one of them arrived! This is so weird!"

There was no doubt in my mind whatsoever that God effectively began saying through my thoughts, *"Maybe I will remember it, because...."* It seemed God had taken special interest in giving me a reason to remember and write exactly as I am writing.

Another thing I had surmised in considering, "God has not given us a spirit of fear, but of power, and of love, and of a sound mind," was that the thing to do to combat a spirit of fear, was the affirmation of this verse, but to say it in full first, "God has not given us a spirit of fear, but of power, and of love, and of a sound mind," then to eliminate reference to the negative, and say, "God has given us a spirit of power, and of love, and of a sound mind." And then repeat that positive portion as many times as I felt good about repeating it.

And do the entire verse the same way later, the next time I felt it appropriate to address the subject. The idea of repeating the whole verse is, first of all, out of respect for God's Word, and secondly, to start honestly with the complete picture. The idea of dropping the reference to fear is out of respect to the part of the verse that tells what God has already given us, and out of appreciation to celebrate what He has done.

*****

How We Bless God Using Faith, Hope, and Love:

How do we bless God? Praising, thanking, obeying, loving. Some of the ways sort of run together. All of those things are to our benefit, as is simply acknowledging God, and when we do them, we are agreeing with the truth and agreeing with God. Let's mostly address obeying for now. When we obey Him, we honor Him. When we obey Him, we are saying we believe Him, and we are agreeing with Him that it is best to do what He says. Dr. Charles Stanley said, "God always honors our obedience to Him."

Remember, God has given us a spirit of power, and of love, and of a sound mind. So instead of waiting around to play defense, go on offense, remembering you have the world's best offense when you let love have the ball, with faith and hope clearing a path for love. Start the day trying to find something to obey God about. Hey, if God is going to honor it, it could pay off big time. Try all day long to come up with things to obey Him about. On the spot. See what might happen. The standard course in the distant past might have been to see what we can get away with. But Numbers 32:23, says, "...be sure your sin will find you out." My maternal grandmother, Mama Barnes, quoted that quite a few times. But instead of trying to get what you can get and trying to get away with it, do the opposite. Search out ways to honor God, by finding things to be obedient about and enjoy the reward that is better than the sin and the cost of sin.

Okay, want some ideas on things to obey Him about? How about adultery? I know, you are thinking that one is too easy. How about this, Jesus said when you look on a woman to lust after her you have committed adultery in your heart already. And I am told that either gender could commit adultery in the heart. Try this. First just because you notice someone's beauty does not mean you choose to lust. God created the beautiful one, and created you to appreciate beauty, inside and out, and that is not sin. But having noticed beauty, look away. You say you have let yourself get conditioned otherwise? No problem. Whether you are a fan of the song "Dixie" or not, seek opportunities like this, and whenever you realize you need to look away, sing in your head, "…look away, look away, look away Dixieland." Continue singing the song for a short while. So simple but so effective, and having done that successfully, you have just blessed God by being obedient, and you can't out-bless God, so congratulations on the blessings that will be coming your way.

That was just one example. Make a regular practice of looking for good ways to play offense, because that is the quickest way to score the most touchdowns. When you look for ways to be obedient to God, you will be investing in blessing God, so a high return on investment is guaranteed. Meanwhile, remember God has already given you the greatest present anyone could give, and the following poem by a little girl in the second grade tells the story in pure glory.

Christmas Poem

Most children like to receive,
But it is more blessed to give.
God gave the best gift of all.
He died so we could live.

His Son was born on Christmas Day
So very long ago.
The Wise Men followed a shining star
That showed them where to go.

His mother named Him Jesus
As God told her to do.
He loves the little children
And that's including YOU!

by Robyn Ivey, 2nd grade, 1991

Published in the Monthly Bulletin of Rehoboth Baptist Church

Chapter 5:
The Song Was Not About Me

In chapter three I wrote:

For several days, a song had been going through my head. The words repeatedly were, "I been cheated, been mistreated, when will I be loved?" It wasn't true. Not for me. I am very loved. I guess I just liked the tune. I don't remember any more of the words, but I really do like the tune. It ran through my head in class, and I began thinking about love. Everybody in the world is loved. Everybody.

I had the wrong perspective. "I been cheated, been mistreated, when will I be loved?" Just as we all relate to the hero in a movie, with this song played over and over in my head, I naturally assumed it was me I was singing about. It wasn't. God has been cheated, been mistreated, when will He be loved? How many people never even acknowledge Him, much less love Him? I revered Him. I respected Him. I appreciated Him. I often acknowledged Him. I spent time with Him. But did I really, really love Him? I considered Him awesome; I couldn't imagine the world without Him. Rather, I sure wouldn't want to imagine being in such a world. I certainly appreciated what He did for my salvation. But did I really, really love Him? As much as I should? I don't think so. Not that much.

In retrospect, I think the words of the song that I was singing in my head, over and over again, may have been Him calling those words to me. Or, if it wasn't Him, He was surely entitled to. I needed to hear them, from Him.

In writing these chapters, I began to think about it. Somehow, many manly men don't seem to express love so well. Can I, with all my imperfections, presume to tell the Creator of the universe I love Him? I stand in awe, but most of the time I am not thinking about Him, and is my awe love? It's not. But at times I have been aware of deep love for Him. So yes, I can boldly come to the Throne of Grace and cry "Abba Father, I love You."

I count February 1, 1981 as my spiritual birthday. Sometime before that I had asked God for help. I told Him I didn't know whether or not He existed, but I needed help. My life was a mess, and I couldn't cope. I was aware of John 3:16 KJV saying, "For God so loved the world, that he gave his only begotten son, that whosoever believed in him should not perish, but have everlasting life." But I didn't really understand what it meant. I told God I just didn't know if He even existed, but I needed help. I told God that if He is real, then I honestly believe in Jesus. I told Him that if God didn't exist, then it didn't matter whether I believed or not. But I cried out to God to help me. And therefore, not knowing whether or not God existed, I believed it enough to cry out to Him for help, and somehow I truly expected Him to help me. And He did. If you wandered or wondered into this book by mistake, welcome. If you want to know whether God exists or not, ask Him and He will show you. He stands at the door and knocks. Just invite Him in, and ask Him.

On January 31, 1981 it rained and a long drought was broken. That same day, coincidently (?), I decided to go to church the next morning. Formerly the owner of an Arabian horse farm and controller of a multi-billion dollar bank and bank holding company, I had not been inside a church in years. I now lived in a lonesome apartment in Roswell, Georgia, and so I looked in the phone book and found Roswell First Methodist Church. I wanted to make it easy on myself, so I told them my address and I asked them if they could give me directions to the *nearest* Methodist Church. They didn't, because years later I learned there was one about a block from the apartment, just in the opposite direction from the direction I traveled. But they gave me directions to their church. Going to their church was a step in the plan God had for me.

When I got there for Sunday School, I didn't know where to go. I went down a hall and a couple was coming out of an office, so they must be pretty official folks, and I asked them where I should go. The lady said, "Come with us, we will take you." They just took me to their Sunday School class.

There was a guest speaker, or she may have been a member of the class, who told of the time, when she was a small girl, she saw her grandmother's arm get mangled in a machine. As I listened, I visualized me as a little boy and my own grandmother and how she would look with her arm mangled in that situation. My grandmother was the most warm-hearted woman anyone could ever be, yet she was a woman of immense internal strength. I spent summers and Christmas vacations working on Grandpa's dairy farm. She let me take the bus to town every Saturday. Grandpa believed "picture shows" were a bad influence. But my grandmother (Mamie Cannon Ivey) knew how much I loved the cowboy heroes, Roy Rogers, Gene Autry, The Lone Ranger and such, so she covered for me. Grandpa didn't have to know.

I didn't realize then how fortunate I was to be under her influence, but in retrospect she was the "love" that made my own Daddy the kindest man I ever knew. She told me of the time when Daddy was a little boy, and how he cried because he accidentally killed an ant. I now so look forward to seeing her in heaven and telling her how much I love her. I was too young to understand such things then - such things as her love. In retrospect, she always was love, so I just took her love for granted.

The speaker told how she, as a little girl, watched as her grandmother prayed and the arm straightened out and became healed right in front of her eyes. There were some other circumstances that caused me to be in that class that day. It was not an accident. After class, the guest speaker and the teacher were talking and I went up to them and said, "I feel like a nut, because I believed every word you said." I have never been accused of being smart socially.

The teacher was a member of the Gideons, who worked for IBM, and he invited me to lunch. His name was, of all things, John Cross. When we had lunch, he led me to the Lord, and I accepted Jesus as my Savior. As we finished, he gave me a Gideons Bible, underlining the words of Proverbs 3: 5 & 6 KJV, "Trust in the Lord with all thy heart; and lean not unto thine own understanding. In all thy ways acknowledge him, and he shall direct thy paths." My memory for names is not good, so God sent a man whose name I could not forget, "John Cross," in accepting what Jesus did for me on the cross. Though I am a CPA, my memory is not so good for numbers either, and, God had John Cross underline, "In all thy ways acknowledge him, and he shall direct thy paths," because "3:6" is a reference I cannot forget, since 3/6, March 6, is my birthday.

Two years later, the wedding present John Cross and his wife gave Francie and me was a plaque that displayed the words of "The Love Chapter." Everyone should study those words. (The exhibit right after Chapter Three is a picture of the plaque.)

What God did in 1981 was about God and His love. God goes to great lengths, with many details, for His children. The words of the song at the beginning of this chapter, "I been cheated, been mistreated, when will I be loved?" were from God, addressing how poorly I had been relating to Him lately. The pleasantness of the tune was about God and how He relates to me, with love.

I always liked the Kris Kristofferson song, "Why me Lord?" It may be about the best Gospel song ever adopted for secular music. Go to the inter net and check it out. Right now. Does it imply that 'lovin' the Lord is a gift to us? Not to the Lord, but to us?

Of course it is not the Bible, saying what it says right there, and maybe I'm wrong, but I think it hits the nail on the head. I don't deserve to love God. My 'lovin' God is a gift from Him to me. Loving the Lord first requires faith, and Romans 10:17 says, "So then faith comes by hearing, and hearing by the *Word of God*."

So no man can boast about his faith, *or his love for the Lord,* both are a gift from God -because the love requires the faith - and the faith first requires the Word of God. Ephesians 2:8-10 says:

> For by grace you have been saved through faith, and that not of yourselves; *it is* the gift of God, not of works, lest anyone should boast. For we are His workmanship, created in Christ Jesus for good works, which God prepared beforehand that we should walk in them."

Notice, we are His workmanship, and He is still growing us, for us to do good things. So read the Bible, and ask Him to help you love Him. Ask Him for the gift. He wants to give you the gift of loving Him.

Psalm 116:1-10:

Thanksgiving for Deliverance from Death

> I love the LORD, because He has heard
> My voice *and* my supplications.
> Because He has inclined His ear to me,
> Therefore I will call *upon Him* as long as I live.
> The pains of death surrounded me,
> And the pangs of Sheol laid hold of me;
> I found trouble and sorrow.
> Then I called upon the name of the LORD:
> "O LORD, I implore You, deliver my soul!"
> Gracious *is* the LORD, and righteous;
> Yes, our God *is* merciful.
> The LORD preserves the simple;
> I was brought low, and He saved me.
> Return to your rest, O my soul,
> For the LORD has dealt bountifully with you.
> For You have delivered my soul from death,
> My eyes from tears,
> *And* my feet from falling.
> I will walk before the LORD
> In the land of the living.
> I believed, therefore I spoke,
> "I am greatly afflicted."

My observation: The sincerest thanksgiving is thanks-living.

The words of the Kris Kristofferson song "Why Me Lord?" will always bring warm and deep feelings to me. Kris Kristofferson sang the words like he meant them. And that made all the difference in the world.

Now, as we all probably have some sort of regrets and deep feelings from mistakes in years gone by, can an elderly person find salvation? Jesus gave us a clue in Matthew 18:3, when he said, "…unless you are converted and become as little children, you will by no means enter the kingdom of heaven."

But he wasn't referring to a literal age requirement, He was referring to the lovable trusting dependence that accompanies being spiritually minded. And you are never too old to come to Him.

For years I had prayed for my mother's salvation, as did others. On August 8, 1988, three days after the completion of the forty-day fast, the family was at Mother and Daddy's house, and I gathered everybody in a circle to pray. Wouldn't hurt to put out a whole net even though Mother was the one fish I had a burden for. Mother was not someone who could be pinned-down to the truth one on one. Her mind was too quick and her spirit was too strong. But maybe leading her to the Lord, leading her to literally say that she accepted Jesus' free gift of her salvation for which Jesus paid the price of being crucified, maybe that was the purpose of the fast!

When I finished the words, with everyone holding hands and repeating after me, and I said amen, Mother, of all people, quickly spoke up. She immediately said, "I said the words, but I haven't done anything wrong!"

What a let-down. The words I wanted her to confess in her heart are found in various chapters throughout this book, words acknowledging that all have sinned and come short of the Glory of the God, and that God so loved us He sent Jesus to pay our sin debt in full. But as Brother Tom says, "You have to get someone lost before you can get them saved." I had no power left in me to push forward. No man can save anyone, it takes the prodding and convicting of the Holy Spirit, and it just wasn't going to happen. Not that day.

Years later, the morning Daddy passed away, I immediately called from the hospital and told Wanda (a wonderful care-giver who had been staying daily twelve hour shifts with Mother and Daddy for several years) what had happened, but I told her not to tell Mother, that I would tell her when I got home. Daddy was ninety-one years old and he was always easy to love, he loved the Lord, as did Wanda, and Wanda loved him, and she was now sad. She took out her Bible and started reading. Then she did something she had tried to do many times before. She went into Mother's room and asked if she could read to Mother from the Bible. In the past

Mother had always rebuffed her. Mother, now weak in body and spirit, though still with a sound mind, agreed and then at the age of 91 about a half hour after Daddy passed away, not even knowing Daddy had gone, she accepted Jesus as her Savior.

NOTE: Mother and Daddy had caregivers in their home 24/7. Wanda Pyant had a nurse's degree, and could have taken a job earning more money, but she came to work for us and stayed with us for years, at the same lower pay scale that the other caregivers received. Was it a coincidence that the right person, with the right heart, with a Bible was in the right place at the right time for Emily Barnes Ivey? No. *God, thank You for answering our prayers. Thank You for sending Wanda.*

<3 <3 <3 <3

There is a wonderful Statler Brothers song titled "Feeling Mighty Fine". You should check it out. It is really good. And I woke up one morning feeling mighty fine, about two a.m., and I had some special memories and ideas on my mind. My grandmother, and love, and seeds, and seeds germinating, and flowers growing. I lay there, considering whether to write down the thoughts from what I may have just dreamed, or whether to go back to sleep. I chose the former. Thinking about my grandmother, and her love of many years ago, and picturing her in that

Sunday School class at Roswell First Methodist Church, and the

pressure I had been under at that time, and me "believing."

From the Bible's love chapter we have learned, "Love ...

> is patient,
> is kind,
> and is not jealous:
> does not brag and is not arrogant.
> Does not act unbecomingly;
> does not seek it's own (not self-seeking)
> is not provoked
> does not take into account a wrong suffered.
> Does not rejoice in unrighteousness, but rejoices with the truth;
> Bears all things,
> Believes all things,
> Hopes all things,
> Endures all things.
> Love never fails..."

Love believes all things? What's that all about? Does it include

acknowledging God in what would seem to others to be coincidences,

when in fact they are the Shepherd's voice? His sheep know His voice,

but only the ones who hear Him call in that particular way would fully

trust it to be Him. I have asked myself, is it like a love letter that should

be considered private between the two? But David showed just the

opposite in such matters, and with David's encouragement, in God's

Word, the answer is to proclaim all God's works. Anyone would surely have to be careful in this area, and in general consider it as just a message saying, "Hi, I am with you always, and I love you."

Maybe, just maybe, seeds of love are planted throughout our lives. Like by my grandmother. And at some point later in life the seeds start to break open, and the life of the flower begins. Maybe the seed has to come under pressure, somehow, and the Holy Spirit is on hand, so that when that time comes, the Lord's love combines with the seeds of love in our soul, and our spirit leads us to believe, one way or another, and at that time we begin a marvelous journey. The Journey requires patience, as something happens over a period of time, and our soul goes through pain of sorts, as the soul tries to sort it all out. It requires kindness, as the walls of the seed are broken open with kindness. The seed has now become more experienced in life, and empathy blossoms. God is growing us. We experience feelings that we don't understand. We do understand at the same time that something's not right, but everything's alright. We have experienced the wrongness of unrighteousness and its fruit and the rightness of truth and its fruit. We have born things, and in hope believed, and endured. We have a decision to make, whether or not, having been so prepared, not understanding life, and seeking to absorb something we can hold onto, a choice comes into view before us, the result of all of our being here on earth, shall we choose spiritual life?

God set before us a choice. He said He hoped we would choose good. He said the choice was between good and evil. Life and death.

When He made Adam, He said, "It is good." But that was before Adam sinned. Then He set before us the choice of being carnally minded or spiritually minded. And the choice of accepting His gift of salvation, since, "All have sinned and come short of the glory of God." In law, including IRS, when someone offers you a gift the property does not become your property until you accept the gift. You can't have what God offers unless you accept it. In contract law, the same principle applies. If God signs a contract saying He promises you something if you sign the contract, the contract is no good unless you sign it.

In personal property law an oral contract is as legal as a written contract, the writing of it is in order to help everybody remember what the contract says, and to give evidence of the agreement. But the agreement, the contract, exists even if it is simply an oral contract. So when God offered Jesus up on the cross, and Jesus gave His life, God had made an offer and fulfilled His part. We complete the gift only when we so indicate by signing the contract, or otherwise accepting the contract.

Technically, in man's law, there can be an implied acceptance, which God would honor also, if it really constitutes acceptance. However, with something so important as the immortal soul, I cannot envision any reason to risk all by not literally, consciously, overtly, and in pure fact, saying "Yes, Lord." Anyway, I think the point of all this writing is that LOVE is sown throughout our lives, first into us, and later from us. So? So now that we know love, it's time to sow love.

It came to my mind immediately after I had written the words "So? So" - but don't let this story distract you from the truth of what is written above - when I was a little boy, I had a dog named SoSo. He was great! He was a Boston Terrier and he could jump so high. I honestly thought that if there were an Olympics for dogs he would win the gold medal in high jumping.

SoSo was hit by a car and killed. The lady next door had a dogwood tree and she offered to let me, a terribly sad little boy, bury SoSo under her dogwood tree. I thought that was marvelous. We had a ceremony, in her back yard, under her tree, and she was there with us. In retrospect, I don't remember even seeing that lady except that one time. But she showed kindness, and she did sow it. So? She was touched, and sowed a spirit of kindness. Kindness is a flower of love. Sow it.

"That which ye *sow, so* shall ye reap" (emphasis mine). Hey, I didn't realize until now, my little dog is in the Bible. Way to go SoSo, they spelled your name 'sow, so' but that's o.k., you are in the Bible. You *really* jumped high!

But then a little boy's gold medal winning Boston Terrier dog buried beneath a dog*wood would.*

Now say this three times real fast: "The lady saw I loved SoSo so much, so she sowed."

Chapter 6:
Why Is Life So Hard?

Why is life so hard? Why do we have to have pain? I don't know. Next question. Seriously, we have to fall back on Proverbs 3:5 KJV, sometimes, "Trust in the Lord with all thine heart; and lean not unto thine own understanding." When a little child has to have surgery, he needs to trust that his parents are doing something good *for* him, not doing something bad *to* him.

The following passages show Jesus trusting His father during times in which Jesus was about to pay the price for our sins.

Matthew 26: 36-56:
Then Jesus went with them to a place called Gethsemane; and he said to his disciples, "Sit here while I go over there and pray." He took with him Peter and the two sons of Zebedee, and began to be grieved and agitated. Then he said to them, "I am deeply grieved, even to death; remain here, and stay awake with me." And going a little farther, he threw himself on the ground and prayed, "My Father, if it is possible, let this cup pass from me; yet not what I want but what you want." Then he came to the disciples and found them sleeping; and he said to Peter, "So, could you not stay awake with me one hour? Stay awake and pray that you may not come into the time of trial; the spirit indeed is willing, but the flesh is weak." Again he went away for the second time and prayed, "My Father, if this cannot pass unless I drink it, your will be done." Again he came and found them sleeping, for their eyes were heavy. So leaving them again, he went away and prayed for the third time, saying the same words. Then he came to the disciples and said to them, "Are you still sleeping and taking your rest? See, the hour is at hand, and the Son of Man is betrayed into the hands of sinners. Get up, let us be going. See, my betrayer is at hand."

While he was still speaking, Judas, one of the twelve, arrived; with him was a large crowd with swords and clubs, from the chief priests and the elders of the people. Now the betrayer had given them a sign, saying, "The one I will kiss is the man; arrest him." At once he came up to Jesus and said, "Greetings, Rabbi!" and kissed him. Jesus said to him, "Friend, do what you are here to do." Then they came and laid hands on Jesus and arrested him. Suddenly, one of those with Jesus put his hand on his sword, drew it, and struck the slave of the high priest, cutting off his ear. Then Jesus said to him, "Put your sword back into its place; for all who take the sword will perish by the sword. Do you think that I cannot appeal to my Father, and he will at once send me more than twelve legions of angels? But how then would the scriptures be fulfilled, which say it must happen in this way?" At that hour Jesus said to the crowds, "Have you come out with swords and clubs to arrest me as though I were a bandit? Day after day I sat in the temple teaching, and you did not arrest me. But all this has taken place, so that the scriptures of the prophets may be fulfilled." Then all the disciples deserted him and fled.

Luke 22:63-65:
Now the men who held Jesus mocked Him and beat Him. And having blindfolded Him, they struck Him on the face and asked Him, saying, "Prophesy! Who is the one who struck You?" And many other things they blasphemously spoke against Him.

In my mind I visualized a conversation with the Lord. I told Jesus, life is hard. He said, "Tell me about it! How long was it you hung on the cross with nails driven through your hands?" He said, "You want to hear about pain? Did you ever sweat large drops like blood falling to the ground, absolutely knowing you were willingly going to be crucified and die for other people's sins?" Then he asked me if I remembered the good times in the past and if I wanted the good times He has arranged for me in the future. I said, "Oh yes, definitely." And He told me He loved me.

Clearly God is growing us. A seed has to die to itself and break

open for a flower to grow. A caterpillar gives forth a butterfly. God loves

us more than any flowers or butterflies. He died for us, not for flowers or butterflies. So if we have to go through a process while we are here on earth, it is a process that will have us rejoicing for eternity. At age seventy now, and with leukemia in remission for more than two years, I can better see this life is but a blink of an eye compared to the future eternity with God. And that future looks good with the promises of verses like 1 Corinthians 2:9.

> **But as it is written:**
> *"Eye has not seen, nor ear heard,*
> *Nor have entered into the heart of man*
> *The things which God has prepared for those who love Him."*

We should be praising God and thanking Him even when we, His children, perceive bad happening to us, as well as the good. Proverbs 3:5 means what it says, and God does not violate a trust. And Romans 8:28 means what it says also. We don't have to praise Him *for* the bad things, but we need to praise Him *in* the bad things. Take heart because God will use that bad for our good.

Romans 8:28 does not say, "All *good* things work together for good to those who love the Lord and are the called according to His purpose." It says, *all* things, meaning the bad things work together for good to us also.

74

Likewise, James 1:2-4 gives comforting encouragement during hard times:

> My brethren, count it all joy when you fall into various trials, knowing that the testing of your faith produces patience. But let patience have its perfect work, that you may be perfect and complete, lacking nothing.

> Do you know why you have bigger problems than do other people? It's because everybody does. When something is up close, it is bigger. Or rather it is bigger to us. And our problems are up close to us. The bigger the problem, the closer we hold it. God already knows how big the storm is. Talk to Him about it anyway. Then tell the storm how big your God is!

In 2002, I was diagnosed with leukemia. Doctor Moore said we would delay chemotherapy for as long as we could, because the more the chemotherapy is used the less effective it tends to become.

In July 2005, the lymph cell count had grown to 36. It continued to grow and by May 2007 was between 70 and 80. Normal is 1.2 to 3.5. We needed to begin the chemotherapy. I had kept the leukemia private until now but now was the time to tell the folks at Bible Fellowship Class at Rehoboth, and ask for prayer.

James 5:15 KJV: "And the prayer of faith shall save the sick, and the Lord shall raise him up..."

When I told the Class about the chemotherapy, Bill Cantrell was the teacher, and his wife, Lynda, asked if that meant I would lose my hair. I had read up on it. The literature said, "Some people lose some hair." That might suggest then that some other people do not lose some hair. Francie read that when the hair grows back, it sometimes grows back a different texture and/or color. I joked in class that she seemed to be looking forward to the idea of being married to a curly-haired red-headed man, and that if I had known what my good-looking woman wanted, I would have started chemotherapy long ago. She countered though, that that wasn't what she wanted, but it would be better than not having me at all. That deflated my joke, but added to my appreciation of her.

The chemotherapy had to be delayed because at the same time, all of a sudden I needed sinus surgery. So the chemotherapy didn't start until August 2007. By then, the lymph count had inexplicably (James 5:15) dropped to 43. Normal is less than 4, so we started the chemotherapy anyway. At the end of the first round of chemotherapy, the lymph count went back to the normal range, and has stayed there, with this being written in October 2009 (James 5:15).

When I was first diagnosed, I read somewhere that there is no cure for the disease. Subsequently a doctor told me that if it stays in remission for five years, one is considered cured.

When Bob spoke from his wheel chair, with ALS, with braces on his wrists because the muscles were gone, he spoke of the movie, "HUD", in which the lead character, Marlon Brando, said, "You know what? You can't get out of life alive!" Again, the only time we can be sure of is the present moment. I am hoping to reach the five year mark in remission and be "cured," even though there is no cure, but every day is a gift. Every day is a bonus for which each of us should give thanks to the Lord.

> Therefore I ask that you do not lose heart at my tribulations for you, which is your glory. For this reason I bow my knees to the Father of our Lord Jesus Christ, from whom the whole family in heaven and earth is named, that He would grant you, according to the riches of His glory, to be strengthened with might through His Spirit in the inner man, that Christ may dwell in your hearts through faith; that you, being rooted and grounded in love, may be able to comprehend with all the saints what *is* the width and length and depth and height—to know the love of Christ which passes knowledge; that you may be filled with all the fullness of God. Now to Him who is able to do exceedingly abundantly above all that we ask or think, according to the power that works in us, to Him *be* glory in the church by Christ Jesus to all generations, forever and ever. Amen (Ephesians 3:13-21).

Whenever you have a problem, cry out to God. Make problems be reminders to cry out to God in prayer. When we call on God, in the name of the Lord Jesus Christ, we are doing what God wants us to do. When Satan attacks, if we use that to remind us to go to the Lord in prayer, that motivates Satan not to make attacks. So make running to the Lord a habit, crying "Abba Father," and the results will be GOOD.

Jesus gave us what we call "The Lord's Prayer," which can be found in Matthew chapter 6. But that was not to be the only prayer for us to pray. So much of the Bible, including words from Jesus, tells us to pray about specific matters. And remember Psalm 100 says:

> Make a joyful shout to the LORD, all you lands!
> Serve the LORD with gladness;
> Come before His presence with singing.
> Know that the LORD, He *is* God;
> *It is* He *who* has made us, and not we ourselves;
> *We are* His people and the sheep of His pasture.
> Enter into His gates with thanksgiving,
> *And* into His courts with praise.
> Be thankful to Him, *and* bless His name.
> For the LORD *is* good;
> His mercy *is* everlasting,
> And His truth *endures* to all generations.

Joyful. Thanksgiving. Praise.

Do check in with Jesus in Matthew chapter six from time to time. But don't just say the words. Think carefully about the words. For example, in verses 9 through 13 below, before you pray verse twelve, "forgive us our debts, As we forgive our debtors," be sure about what you are asking for. Pray each verse, but if you pray it, mean it, because God might think you want Him to take you at His Word.

> 9. In this manner, therefore, pray: Our Father in heaven, Hallowed be Your name.
> 10. Your kingdom come. Your will be done On earth as *it is* in heaven.
> 11. Give us this day our daily bread.
> *12. And forgive us our debts, As we forgive our debtors,*
> 13. and do not lead us into temptation, But deliver us from the evil one. For Yours is the kingdom and the power and the glory forever. Amen.
> Concerned about how to pray? Don't be. Just be a simple sheep.

Listen for His voice and He will lead you. "My sheep hear My voice, and I know them, and they follow Me." (John 10:27).

Sheep cannot outfight predators. Nor can they outrun predators. And yet, they are in no danger when they are close to the Shepherd.

> These things I have spoken to you, that in Me you may have peace. In the world you will have tribulation; but be of good cheer, I have overcome the world (John 16:33).

A dilemma is a problem without a solution. In Christ, there are no dilemmas. He knows where the Easter eggs are hidden, so when you go on a hunt for solutions, take Him with you.

Oh, and before you go on the hunt, after you ask Him to go with you, go ahead and thank Him for what you asked Him for. If you keep asking Him for the solution, it keeps you tense. If you thank Him for the Easter egg, before you have even see it, somehow, that can help you see it. Keep thanking Him, for Easter eggs asked for but as yet unseen. Somehow, speaking things helps give birth to them.

> Psalm 40:3: He has put a new song in my mouth—
> Praise to our God;
> Many will see *it* and fear,
> And will trust in the LORD.

Psalm 33:3 KJV, "Sing unto him a new song; play skilfully with a loud noise."

'PLAY' skillfully? With a loud noise?

SHAZAM! Flash! This just in. Coming in *loudly* over the air waves now, and it could just as well as not – be - from God -

Yes, the Father should be shown great respect, but sometimes, it seems, He chooses to just enjoy playing with his children. Maybe not most of the time. But sometimes. Yet, even then He is growing us, with love.

> As the hart panteth after the water brooks, so panteth my soul after thee, O God (Psalm 42:1 KJV).

> Delight thyself also in the Lord; and He shall give thee the desires of thine heart (Psalm 37:4 KJV).

I will sing unto the Lord, because He hath dealt bountifully with me (Psalm 13:6).

Definitely praise Him in the good and great times. God wants me to spend time with Him. If I go to Him making requests when life is hard, but say nothing when life is good and great, guess what I am inviting. I am inviting Him to not give me good and great times. When times are good and great, that is the best time to talk to the Lord. Still whenever I have troubles, whenever I need to get out of something, I need to remember:

...Jonah prayed his way out of the belly of a fish

...Paul praised his way out of jail (That's the amazing thing. Praise God when things are bad. I know that can be hard, but know that God inhabits the praise of His people, and where God is, there is joy and peace.)

It's amazing, what praying and praising, can do, when it tells God "I love You!" The closer we get to God, the more it seems like Heaven opens up and blessings so fully flow, and things turn to gold.

And these things write we unto you, that your joy may be full (1 John 1:4 KJV).

And Jacob awaked out of his sleep, and he said, Surely the Lord is in this place... (Gen. 28:16 KJV).

Special appreciation to Rehoboth Bible Fellowship teacher Bill Cantrell:

This seems a good place to say it pleases me to consider that maybe Mr. Cantrell was following the Lord's leading when he quoted in class my "letters to the editor" from newspapers, and letters to him, and a few times exclaimed that I should write a book. His comments helped me to consider that maybe I could write a book if I simply write about real life things I feel a burden to write about - like I did with the letters - plus, with the book, I would write things I wanted to pass down to my children, grandchildren, and anyone who would listen.

I know it is not necessary at all, but if it were necessary to prevent a spirit of pride from creeping in, I would remind my dear friend, Mr. Cantrell, and me, that Numbers 22 shows that omnipotent God can even cause words to come from the mouth of a donkey. So at *best*, that's how proud we should be. Oh, and one more thing. I suspect that AFTER that donkey spoke to Balaam, then all he could do was go around saying, "He Haw! He Haw! He Haw!" But I suspect it was the most joyful He Hawing he had ever done.

Chapter 7:
"Dem Bones Dem Bones Dem Dry Bones"

"In the beginning was the Word, and the Word was with God and the Word was God" (John 1:1).

"And the Word was made flesh, and dwelt among us, and we beheld His glory (the glory as of the only begotten of the Father) full of grace and truth" (John 1:14).

I once had a Sunday School teacher who said, "You can't overestimate God. So always *try* to let any error be on the side of overestimating Him, otherwise you will underestimate Him."

I believe that. God astonishes me, only because I do underestimate Him.

The song "Dem Bones Dem Bones Dem Dry Bones" by the Rhythm Boys simply goes through the anatomy of the body, bone by bone, "connected to the" and from time to time it says: "Now hear the Word of the Lord." That's all it does, and yet it is a wonderful song, with a very enjoyable rhythm and tune. It refers to Ezekiel 37:1-6:

> The hand of the LORD came upon me and brought me out in the Spirit of the LORD, and set me down in the midst of the valley; and it *was* full of bones. Then He caused me to pass by them all around, and behold, *there were* very many in the open valley; and indeed *they were* very dry. And He said to me, "Son of man, can these bones live?"
> So I answered, "O Lord GOD, You know." Again He said to me, "Prophesy to these bones, and say to them, 'O dry bones, hear the

word of the LORD! Thus says the Lord GOD to these bones: "Surely I will cause breath to enter into you, and you shall live. I will put sinews on you and bring flesh upon you, cover you with skin and put breath in you; and you shall live. Then you shall know that I *am* the LORD."

In the song, focus on "Now hear the Word of the Lord..." which is repeatedly sung in wonderful rhythm, but *hear* it because that is the stuff faith is made of. Really. Romans 10:17 says, "So then faith *comes* by hearing, and hearing by the word of God." And if you don't read your Bible every day, how do you have the strength to survive spiritual battles?

Most people eat three meals a day. I don't bother with lunch, except on weekends. I'm just not interested in eating during the work day. And I don't miss it. But there is no way I would want to start the day without reading the Bible. I have had some long fasts of physical food, and it was a healthy thing not a harmful thing. But fasting the Bible is dangerous. The carnal body reminds me to eat physical food, there is no danger that I would ever starve to death by oversight. But my carnal body will never remind me to take spiritual food. I overcome that by the intentional HABIT of reading the Bible every morning. I am doing that with a little daily devotional book, "Jesus Calling," by Sarah Young. Truly the best such book I have ever encountered. Except I have recently added, "You Can Take It With You," by Linda Sommer, and it seems equally powerful, with tremendous variety.

Faith. It comes from the Word of God. There is no other way. And faith is essential in being spiritually minded. Faith is more important than I realize. How can I know that, and not realize how important it is? I know the genealogy of Jesus' mother begins with Abraham, who is called the Father of Faith. In my current condition, if I heard God tell me to sacrifice my son to Him, back then, I don't know how I would ever have been spiritually minded enough to have Faith that God would tell me to do that. And likely, Abraham did not know that in that incident, he was a physical picture of Spiritual God doing the same thing for us. And Abraham's son was a forerunner of Jesus, whose Father sacrificed His Son on the cross, for us. So God will never ask anyone to do that again, because, as Jesus said on the cross, "It is finished!"

Abraham, though, believed God and was willing, and because of his faith he received a blessing that is to last "a thousand generations." Our having faith must be pretty important to God. And if it is that important to God for us to have faith, there is a reason for it. Or, rather, many reasons. I can think of quite a few right now.

Actually, the Bible says, "Without faith, it is impossible to please God." But our faith ebbs and flows. So we MUST get fed from the Word of God daily. Skipping a day might lead to skipping two, or three, or all, and perhaps the spiritual trigger to remind us to come back might have to be some terrible calamity leading us painfully crying out to God. Terrible calamities are not fun.

Jesus said, "If you had the faith of a mustard seed (and He was referring to the tiniest seed in that part of the world at the time) you could move mountains." I would rather move mountains of problems than be a lightening rod for terrible calamities.

Jesus is so important to God, and your accepting what He has done for you is so important to God. And having done that, He would like you to grow spiritually and understand that He has something for you to do for Him right here on earth. You need to be obedient to the extremely helpful rules he has set forth for your own good, and you need to address seriously the principle of love. He has humanly unimaginably wonderful times ahead for you after that.

In a previous chapter I wrote about admitting fear by (1) focusing ON GOD (2) following WITH PRAISE. This morning I tried it, with something *similar* to fear.

I started it at 4:14 a.m. I wanted to get to the office early so I could write from my pencil notes onto the draft of this chapter. I was carrying it in "mail waiting to be sent," on the office computer. But like the other mornings lately, I would probably not get there until a little after 8:30 even though it is only five minutes from home. I started.

"Father, I admit I am feeling a time problem." I start telling Him about the things I want to do. I hear a smile in "our" voice as He says, "May I?" That was a game from my days as a small boy in Hogansville. If you didn't say, "Father, may I," you had to go all the way back to where you started.

And I remembered that as I began to practice *"admitting* fear, focusing *on God*, following *with praise*, I realized I had omitted the "salutes of thanksgiving and praise" that I know to be appropriate near the beginning of talking with Him. I didn't ask, as one would in the military, "Permission to speak, Sir?" God is higher ranking than any military officer, and deserves more respect. Sure, sometimes I can come crying to

Him saying, "Abba, Father" because of His love for me, and I'm already being spiritually minded, but He still deserves the respect of not having a presumptuous son reporting to Him with forgetfulness of proper relationship, when time and emotions will easily allow it.

So I started over, this time coming into the gate thanking God for reminding me, and coming into His court giving Him the well deserved praise. In the simple but penetrating words from Sarah Young, in her book, *Jesus Calling*, when you come to the Lord, "You have nothing to hide and nothing to disclose..." That is because He already knows everything, including your thoughts. But He still wants your thoughts and He still wants to converse with you. Ms. Young made quite an understatement when she provocatively said, "You can have no other relationship like this one."

Remembering we are in the process of practicing *admitting* fear, focusing *on God*, and following with *praise*, I will continue, "Father, it is amazing to consider that I am speaking to the Creator of the universe, the Creator of all that I can see in any direction, and that doesn't even begin to describe what You have done, as You are in control right here on earth as well as... Father I have a time problem. I guess that is a good thing, as I think about it, because there are so many things I want to do. It's as if I am in an ice cream parlor, and there are so many flavors of ice cream that it will take so much time to taste them all. But I want to taste them all. I know. I can go faster if I slow down, and let You choose what I do next." I have done the saluting and the admitting. And actually, I feel I have some response, because the message to slow down and let Him do the choosing is another way of hearing the words of Proverbs 3:6, "In all your ways acknowledge Him And He shall direct your paths." Now I am going to pause and focus on God. I'll be back in an unhurried moment.

Finished. This will take practice, but we've got all the time in the world.

All the Leaves Have Fallen

All the leaves have fallen
Have fallen to the ground.
I don't know why they did it.
I did not hear a sound.

God made the leaves to grow in spring
and in the Fall fall down.
I feel God's love everywhere
For it is all around

All around.

Words by Francie, music by Robyn, years ago. The music
is quietly and sweetly captivating.

Chapter 8:
What It Was Was Football

Sometimes, words flow so quickly and easily it seems that the result is much better than my ability to write. I know God is in it. Other times, I work very hard writing something that I really want to convey, and the quality is poor and clearly just me. It is at that time that I need to address being carnally minded versus spiritually minded. When God wants to be involved in something, and I expect He just might like to be involved in everything, our carnal nature blocks Him. His Spirit communicates with our spirit, not with our carnal mind. The communication goes from His Spirit to our spirit, to our mind. If we are being carnally minded at the moment, our carnal mind tends to block out spiritual communication, and we miss out on a blessing.

That principle is surely true with things other than writing, but it is easy to realize when writing. The result of writing is before the writer's eyes instantly and he can tell even before he finishes a paragraph whether God is carrying the ball. Being on God's team, I surely don't want to be blocking God. If God wants to carry the ball, and He does, I want to be alert to block *for* Him, not block *Him*.

My Hero

My hero is great.
My hero is strong.
My hero is Jesus
All day long.

That poem was written by me about my hero, who is the only real hero I have. I believe that Jesus died on the cross and rose again. He died for my sins. I love Jesus.

I love Him and
He loves me.
We'll live in heaven
For eternity.

Jesus is the best! I believe that Jesus never sinned. He is everything my poems say. He was born from a virgin. He died on a cross. He rose again. He lives today. "Jesus loves me, this I know, because the Bible tells me so."

He knows everything.
He lives everywhere.
He gave me a talent
For me to share.

Jesus is part of the Trinity: the Father, the Son, and the Holy Spirit. God made us with talents that we should use. Jesus died for our sins so we can go to heaven and that the Holy Spirit can guide us on Earth. The Holy Spirit guides us to be more like the perfect hero, Jesus.

(Robyn Ivey 5th Grade Midvale Elementary 11-8-94)

Chapter 9:
Fearfully and Wonderfully Made

David displayed the right attitude in Psalm 139:14, focusing on God:

> I will praise You, for I am fearfully *and* wonderfully made;
> Marvelous are Your works,
> And *that* my soul knows very well.

Lucifer was magnificent. But his focus was on himself. When he was created, he was perfect. His physical appearance was glorious, as was his music. Did he praise God for that? No. Instead he used his free will to rebel. But he did not possess power equal to God's. It doesn't take the brain of a rocket scientist to know better than to create something that has the free will to rebel as well as the ability to win against you. God wasn't born yesterday. Actually God always has been, is, and always will be. When Lucifer used his free will to let the evil of pride come into his heart, he began a rebellion against God, and tried to take God's throne. The Bible says God then changed Lucifer's name to Satan. I visualize, and this is just me visualizing it, I visualize that was followed by all the evil in the universe swooping in, and being contained into one body. Satan then became the source of all evil. The evil already existed, but now it was "contained", except the Bible says one-third of the angels followed the devil in his rebellion. God banished Satan and the other fallen angels to earth. There would be no evil in heaven. Having visualized as described above regarding Satan and evil, I describe in Chapter 17 a process that I imagine is more likely regarding evil and Satan. But regardless, the end result is the same: God is perfect and good and Satan is horrible and evil. And I think I agree with somebody's description that Satan is not the opposite of God, he is the horrible absence of God.

Before God created us, He prepared that perfect future eternal home for us, heaven. The Bible describes it as being beyond our imagination in its desirability for us. But first, for some reason, to be disclosed by Him in His good timing, we were created to begin life here on earth, the new home of Satan and his demons.

But God didn't just abandon us. No way. He used all for our good, and he went to *great pains* (Jesus crucified on the cross for example) to make that future possible. When God created us, He used His wisdom to create us in such a way that when we do right, it helps us internally. When we praise Him it does something to our brain, our emotions, our soul, something positive. We benefit. When we praise Him, we are telling truth. That does good things for us internally. When we praise Him, when we tell truth, others benefit from truth, and we are being good role models for others, helping others all the more. When we come to Him with praise and thanksgiving we are being spiritually minded and that does tremendously good things for us internally. And surely *Eternally*.

Creating Lucifer/Satan and banishing him from heaven, God rid heaven of evil, and prepared heaven for us. If we didn't experience the presence of evil here on earth, for what amounts to a blink of an eye, we could not as well appreciate the absence of evil in heaven, for eternity.

> Blessed is the man who perseveres under trial, because when he has stood the test, he will receive the crown of life that God has promised to those who love Him (James 1:12).

Man, certainly including me, has no grasp of the wisdom of God, and the things He has done. More significantly, man has no grasp of the love of God. We praise God for both His wisdom and His love, and for so much else, but we really can't grasp it all. God is beyond man's comprehension. The goodness of God is beyond man's comprehension. But the satisfaction to be attained from attempting to comprehend His goodness is a blessing available to all.

I am amazed when I think about the things God has done. And when I think about the Old Testament, I have a view of its depth when I consider a teacher in Bible study at Rehoboth said, "The Old Testament is a physical picture of spiritual truths." I have quoted it more than once. But the wisdom of such a painting, couched in unequaled creativity is beautiful to think about. Genesis 1:1 describes God at work, beginning a priceless painting. "In the beginning God created..." But God didn't finish the painting in that verse, or in Genesis, or in the Old Testament, or in the whole Bible!

When Francie and I were dating, there was a Seven-Eleven store near where I lived, and there was a Magic Market store near where she lived, or vice versa. I kept calling each of them by the wrong name, so we started referring to each as the Seven-Eleven Magic Market. With that formula, I was never wrong.

Bob passed away on Seven-Eleven (7-11-88), and that "coincidence" is one of many things the Lord used to encourage me to complete the forty-day fast, even after the primary reason for the fast, as I understood it, was no longer applicable.

In Isaiah 7:11 (I don't know what year, but it was long before 7-11-88), God spoke to Ahaz and said, "Ask for a sign from the Lord your God..." But Ahaz refused. He was not willing to acknowledge the Lord as his God. When someone is spiritually blind to you, it makes your significance invisible to them. If you were invisible to your children, I mean you were there but they refused to acknowledge you, how would you feel? I expect you would feel very invisible. After awhile, although you loved your children, if they rudely never acknowledged your gifts, you would probably stop giving them things. How do we want God to feel? Whenever you think of the Lord, remember three little words, "I love you" - and remember three big words - "Acknowledge, Acknowledge, Acknowledge!"

God is still painting a priceless picture. You meant something special to someone this past week, whether you knew it or not. Maybe it was when you responded in a way that someone would take heart from and appreciate. But it was a small matter and he/she didn't mention it, or maybe you didn't even realize the Lord had done a good thing through you. Maybe you showed interest in one little thing and someone was encouraged by it. Andy Rooney wrote, "...just one person saying to me, 'You've made my day!' makes my day." Look for the Lord's hand at work through you. And *acknowledge* it. Understand, you may already be a link in a very important chain, even if it is simply sowing seeds.

Need some encouragement? Then let God give it to someone through you, and you will receive it. There is a spiritual principle there. God may want you to practice it. He may want you to walk more closely down that path with Him. Don't be an Ahaz. Practice *acknowledging* the Lord as your God, and God as your Lord.

Jesus rose from the dead, sent the Comforter, and God is still painting a priceless picture. But *now, while He is painting it, His paintbrush is in our hands.*

GOD TEACHES A TEACHABLE SPIRIT!

Francie's Daddy had to go to prison. And I did too. Jesus said, "Follow Me and I will make you fishers of men." For decades now he has been known as "Brother Tom" to thousands of inmates. There are perhaps tens of thousands, who will be rejoicing with him in heaven. He founded Highways and Hedges Christian Ministries, and we went to prison because, as he puts it, "That's where the fish are biting," and I was so blessed to be one small part of it.

It may have been more than twenty years ago now, but Brother Tom took me with him to visit Source of Light Ministries, off I-20, just outside Madison, Georgia. With technological changes, I don't know if they still have a "dark room." I just don't happen to know if technological changes have affected such things. But I would like to share a spiritual lesson I learned that day, on the way to the dark room.

Source of Light produces "Mail Box Club" Bible lessons, and Highways and Hedges buys them from Source of Light, and distributes them by mail, then grades them when they come back, paying postage for students both ways. They are sent to prison inmates and their children after an inmate accepts Jesus as his or her savior, and says he wants them.

It seems to me the Holy Spirit is powerfully at work in the writing of those lessons, with wisdom displayed wonderfully, for simple and practical everyday usage. They seemed to me so meaningful, almost alive. Their truth is beauty.

Jesus said, "I was in prison, and you came to me." And, "Whatsoever you have done unto the least of these, my brethren, you have done also unto me." I don't think many people can be much more "least" than prison inmates and their children. The inmates know Highways and Hedges has no influence with any prison authorities. We have to beg our way into prison, and we are there to serve the Lord and help the inmates spiritually, not to be their advocate with anyone.

Our host at Source of Light led us to the dark room. The route included a special pathway, just a few feet wide. First there was a left turn as we walked in the narrow pathway between two walls. Then there was an extremely sharp right turn, almost a hundred and eighty degrees, then an extremely sharp left turn. It became completely dark. No one had turned off any lights. I remarked that I did not realize light doesn't go around corners. Our host responded, "That's right. And there is a spiritual lesson there somewhere, too." And that's what I want to share.

He didn't elaborate. But I think one principle regarding light is that it goes in a straight line. Sure it bounces off things, but then it goes in a new straight line. I think that is also the way spirits are, good spirits or evil spirits. They can go only in the direction they are headed. They can't change course. Our soul helps adjust the course of our spirit when appropriate. I suspect life here on earth is a process for melding our spirit with our soul. (Some people think spirit and soul are synonymous. So I will address that within the next few pages.)

In football, momentum is frequently significant. The team on a roll is frequently going to stay on a roll until something out of the ordinary causes the momentum to change. In other arenas it is called inertia. In high school I learned in Coach Butch Lee's physics class that inertia is, "The tendency of a moving object to continue moving and the tendency of a stationary object to remain stationary." It will be that way until something interferes and causes it not to happen.

Well, Jesus clearly understood inertia and would have earned an A+ in Coach Lee's physics class. Here is why. Jesus, of course, had always done what God told Him to do. At the end of Jesus' forty-day fast, Satan tried to tempt Jesus. He suggested that Jesus turn stones into bread. What would have been wrong with that? The forty day fast was over. And anyway, God did not say, "Don't take a bite of that stone." Why would turning it into bread be a bad thing? It is because if Jesus had done what Satan suggested, the *inertia*/momentum/*program* of Jesus following His Father would have changed. He would be following the suggestion of Satan rather than God the Father. It worked in the Garden of Eden.

Nobody starts out saying, "I think I will become a terrible criminal." It starts with a little thing, a little thing we do wrong. For most of us, our soul understands and adjusts after we do a wrong thing. We don't let the momentum build. So we don't become a terrible criminal. But what do we become? Left to the world's idea of good, we would become like other un-Godly people. Our soul would consider society in general as the role model. And without the influence of the Holy Spirit, culture would go downhill fast.

But, as somebody said, "God doesn't grade on the curve; He grades on the cross." Once we have sinned (and "All have sinned and come short of the glory of God," per Romans 3:23 KJV), our behavior would perhaps be acceptable to the world, at least for awhile, but not to God, and again without the Holy Spirit, culture would deteriorate, degenerate, fast. Perhaps, but for the grace of God, right now you and I would be terrible criminals. You don't you believe it?

Consider this: Satan exists, otherwise Jesus would not have spoken of him so often. And Satan is more powerful, more cunning, than us. He has a few thousand years experience at tricking people. He is the embodiment of hate that desires to destroy us.

So, the key is to follow Jesus, and try not to take a single baby step toward Satan, lest inertia eventually take hold. As has been said, "Sin will take you further than you want to go, keep you longer than you want to stay, and cost you more than you want to pay." I know that to be true, and I expect you do too. Love God with all your heart, soul and strength. Staying with love, the greatest offense, is better than giving up the ball and playing defense.

Read Isaiah 58:13, 14:

If you turn away your foot from the Sabbath,
From doing your pleasure on My holy day,
And call the Sabbath a delight,
The holy *day* of the LORD honorable,
And shall honor Him, not doing your own ways,
Nor finding your own pleasure,
Nor speaking *your own* words,

Then you shall delight yourself in the LORD;
And I will cause you to ride on the high hills of the earth,
And feed you with the heritage of Jacob your father.
The mouth of the LORD has spoken.

Now think about this. Honoring the Sabbath is a God-built spiritual mechanism for the soul. It helps break the hold of Satan's momentum; it is an inertia tool from the wisdom of God. It reins in the spirit. It rests, recharges, and refuels the soul and its influence with the spirit. God gives us tools like the Sabbath because He loves us. How long has it been since you told Him you love Him back? Now is always a good time to do it again.

And when you do slip and mess up, quicker than you would pull your hand out of a fire, confess to the Lord what you just did, and stop the momentum by turning and going in the other direction, meaning "repent". But praise God for the wonderful things He has done in your life because you just knocked down a pass on fourth down, and now you are back on offense again. You will score a lot more points if you stay on offense. Don't fumble the ball, but if you do, cover it with the blood of Jesus Christ as quickly as possible, and it's your ball again. Love God, and don't forget that you do.

The following is just a silly little poem I wrote about when the focus is on Jesus versus on me.

"My 'i''S..."
(BY BiLL iVEY)

A. How to get somewhere:

My eye's on the Shepherd,
AS i SEEK HIS FACE
And He just leads me
AT HIS JUST RIGHT PACE.

B. How to get nowhere:

My eyes on me,
IN A MAZE I RACE
My eyes off Him,
AND HIS AMAZING GRACE
My...I's...in trouble!
I JUST RUN IN PLACE!

God prefers to drink out of a clean cup:

Dr. Richard Lee said, "God prefers to drink out of a clean cup."

And He does. I agree 100%. But sometimes it seems like about the only

time I am a clean cup is when I've just confessed my sin to the Lord, and

I am thereby immediately cleaned up by the blood of Jesus. In our

polluted cultural environment, it seems like I get at least a little bit dirty in

just a little bit of time. I know my thoughts become less than Holy when I

forget about the Lord. Long ago, I thought that since I had done wrong,

God would not want to use me. How wrong that attitude is.

The cleanest folks can let pride sneak into their hearts, and as Lucifer learned the hard way, or maybe the problem was he refused to learn, pride is not something God will tolerate. (I'm reminded of the country song, "Lord, it's hard to be humble when you're perfect in every way." But it was just in fun, with the same point, just tongue in cheek.) Anyway, it seems like the least good person, calling on the name of Jesus, is cleaner in the eyes of God, than the otherwise most good person who has pride for his otherwise goodness. We are never too dirty for the Lord to clean us up. And He is ready to work with you and me right now. Why? Because He loves you and me. Let's return the favor. Let's love Him with all our heart and everything we've got. And tell him about it.

Another pop song - one from when I was a boy - "Oh have you talked to the Man upstairs, 'cause He wants to hear from you." It doesn't seem to me that "the Man upstairs" is a proper reference to Almighty God, but for those who are just learning, it is a whole lot better than nothing. God does want to hear from you. He wants to hear from you. All the time. I may be wrong, but I think Jesus said what He meant, and meant what He said in Luke 18:1 KJV, "...men ought always to pray..."

That is certainly not a direct order, or a commandment. It is just good advice. One teacher said He meant always be in a *spirit* of prayer.

Another said He meant, always *"keep an open line to Him."* Those answers come because of the seeming impossibility of doing exactly what Jesus said do. And the perceived impossibility of doing exactly what Paul said do, when Paul said "Pray without ceasing." In fact, in 1 Thessalonians 5:16-18 he said, "Rejoice always, **pray without ceasing**, in everything give thanks; for this is the will of God in Christ Jesus for you."

But consider this. When Jesus saved the adulterous woman from being stoned, He then told her, in John 8:11, "Go and sin no more," and likely she ceased adultery, but one would suspect that she in fact did commit some little sin in the remainder of her whole life. If she didn't, she was a better man than I am.

Still, it seems the mission Jesus set before her was to sin no more. Perhaps it is the same with, "praying always." Maybe that really is the mission Jesus clearly set before us. Why? Because being perfect, Jesus seeks for us to be perfect, and we should also. It would be to our benefit, and to the benefit of those to whom we minister. He loves us, and wants what is best for us.

The adulterous woman probably tried to sin no more. And by trying, she probably came a lot closer than she would have if she had not tried at all. Perhaps her real mission was like what my "other grandmother," Mama Barnes, who had come to live with us, always said to us kids as we left the house, "Be good. And if you can't be good, be good as you can." She should be given credit for publicizing the positive *goal* of being good, and doing so with good humor. Jesus just set the bar higher than that, in order to get the highest result possible, and if we can't quite make it, we can retain our humility, which would be a wonderful result. So, believing Jesus and Paul meant what they said, I am in the boat with the country preacher who said, "If a literal reading of the Bible makes good sense, don't try to make any other kind of sense out of it." I hope it is not a boat that tips over real easily.

Again, praying always is not a commandment, like loving God with everything we've got is a commandment, but it is divine advice that we should not ignore. Greater men than me believe it should not be taken literally. So maybe I'm wrong. But I promise you, even if I am wrong, I do better in life when I try to pray always.

RELATING TO GOD

You can't love God if you don't know Him at all.
You can't know God at all if you don't have any faith at all that He exists.
If you have faith that God exists, you can know Him.
If you know Him, you will love Him.

Faith and love grow over time, if they are not neglected.
If they are neglected, they can be renewed, though the lost time cannot be regained.
But they can be renewed with earnest, thereby compensating for some lost time.
But don't count on it.
There are times when God says, "That's enough. I will not abide your behavior, nor will I pursue you any longer."
That is not necessarily the end. God can respond to being urged to change His position. Sometimes.
To get to know God better, and to touch His heart, spend time with Him.
Those who appreciate the Son gain approval from the Father.
As you go through the day, try to stay conscious of Jesus.
But you will need some reminders.

Acknowledge Reminders:

When you receive reminders, acknowledge to Him that they are from Him! You cannot overestimate God!

A tempting thought just flew by? Maybe temptation to worry? If a bird flies over your head, that is not sin. If you let it build a nest in your hair - that is sin. Thank the Lord for reminding you to notice it, to reject it, and praise Him for His ability to remind you. Let a bird flying over your head, or a hint of temptation, be a reminder to go to the Lord thanking Him for the reminder. Let the reminder draw you closer to the Lord. He loves to give reminders IF we will acknowledge them and Him.

I acknowledge God inspired me to write about acknowledging reminders and Him:

Acknowledge them and Him,
Give thanks and give praise.
That will lighten up and brighten up
the fullness of your days!
And it will touch the heart of God.

Francie acknowledges that in the middle of the night God inspired

her to write about God in this poem:

All the leaves have fallen
Have fallen to the ground
I don't know when they did it
I did not hear a sound
God made the leaves to grow in Spring
and in the Fall fall down.
I feel God's presence everywhere
For it is all around
All around

I am reminded of a song from World War II, entitled "You're in the Army Now":

You're in the Army now.
You're not behind the plough.
You'll never get rich
Just digging a ditch.
You're in the Army now!

How much do you know about the Military? In World War II,

Daddy was in the Air Force Engineers, which at that time was a division

of the Army. Coincidently, like me, he was seven years older than his

baby brother. As you can imagine, I have always cherished that "coincidence." And speaking of cherished, one of my most cherished pictures is one I have that shows the two of them, each with one arm around the other's shoulder, standing beside Uncle James' airplane on "Daddy's" airfield. Uncle James was a U. S. Army Air Force pilot. He landed on the airfield that Daddy had just built in North Africa.

I am reminded of the song "Onward Christian Soldiers" and that the military may be a model of how to approach our Commander in Chief, God. But first there are some things to point out. It won't do any good to come to God carnally minded. You won't be able to hear him. Prayer is a two way conversation. So if you are carnally minded, how do you change gears? Easy. Thanksgiving and Praise. Nick Vujicic, a man with no arms and no legs, said, "I never met a thankful man who was bitter. And I never met a bitter man who was thankful."

> Make a joyful noise unto the Lord, all ye lands. Serve the Lord with gladness: come before His presence with singing. Know ye that the Lord He is God: it is He that hath made us, and not we ourselves; we are His people, and the sheep of His pasture. *Enter into His gates with thanksgiving,* and *into His courts with praise*: be thankful unto Him, and bless His name. For the Lord is good; His mercy is everlasting; and His truth endureth to all generations. (Psalm 100 KJV w/some capital letters mine.)

Thanksgiving is an immediate response to something God just did, or something in the past you just remembered, and a spirit of that remembering. It takes place at the gate. Once you are past the gate, praise is the magnet that draws you into the closeness of God. Praise is a spiritual principle and, like thanksgiving, it is a first cousin to the military principle of saluting. Whenever you purposely want to talk to God, you are probably past the gate, and so if you are, give Him a salute of praise. And maybe a lot more than a quick salute. Maybe continue until you feel Him return the salute. Not because he needs it, but because you need to give the praise to acknowledge your right relationship with Him.

In the military, when you report to a higher ranking officer, the relationship is acknowledged with a salute by you. You stand at attention continuing the salute, awaiting his response. He is required, I repeat, military law requires that he return your salute. So when you praise God, I see there a spiritual law, that His ethics require Him to respond to you. I know God is not really 'required' to do anything, but I expect He establishes that as His SOP. (See Psalms 22.) And with you as a son or daughter having given sincere praise, He now is in a position to respond to you. With *you* in a spiritually minded position you can now hear His response.

Psalms 22 tells us that God inhabits the praises of His people. Sarah Young wrote "...a living channel absorbs some of whatever flows through it." She sees us as a channel through which Jesus can comfort others. I see that when Jesus blesses others through us, we are made in such a way that we absorb a blessing. And if we are praising God in spirit and in truth, He is inhabiting the praise, and we are absorbing – Him.

Now might be a good time to go to the Lord in prayer. Now is the time to tell God you love Him.

Prayer continued:

And there is no hurry, and yet you "needs must go." But not yet. Soon, but not yet. You are in the warehouse, where love is stored, and there is no need to leave yet. And there is more coming in, and you feel God's presence all around. All around. You want to leave, because you sense it can't last, yet you linger, *Not so fast.* You stay awhile, and start to smile, knowing just, all the while, an army moves in single file, as you are in the ammunition depot of the Lord's love, and feel His love. And absorb His love. Love coming from Him, through you. Praise Him for He is love. Abide in His love. Linger in His presence as His love flows through you to Him in appreciation of this moment. Allow the One who shed His blood for you to flow through your blood, and feel the cleansing of His Spirit flowing through, as you just say, "Thank You. And I love You." And cherish the moment. And desire to return to it. Look forward to returning to it, yet while the moment still lingers as you linger in His arms, more and more is being stored up, and your strength has no measure and no challenge, and all the while love has a smile, hugs, and a hint of tears of sweetness. You don't want to leave the love depot. Linger. Awhile.......

> Blessed *be* the God and Father of our Lord Jesus Christ, the Father of mercies and God of all comfort, who comforts us in all our tribulation, that we may be able to comfort those who are in any trouble, with the comfort with which we ourselves are comforted by God (2 Cor. 1: 3-4).

> When you go to the love depot, remember, "a living channel absorbs some of whatever flows through it."

Who makes mistakes?
And two keys............

What do you do when you make a mistake? What do you do when someone else makes a mistake?

I suspect Scott Hudgens went to the Love Depot more than a time or two. I first started out in public accounting while I was still in college. To be a CPA in Georgia at that time, you had to pass the CPA exam, have a college degree in accounting, and you had to have, after the age of twenty-one, two years experience under the supervision of a CPA. I wanted to become a CPA at the youngest age legally possible, and I did it. Part of doing it was going to work for our (my parents') next door neighbor, CPA Otis Childs.

I was the only one in the office one day when our largest client, Scott Hudgens, called. In later years, Scott Hudgens became a household word in Atlanta real estate; he became a multi-millionaire and a Christian philanthropist. He asked me an easy tax question, and I gave him the answer. After we hung up, I got to thinking about it, and looked up the answer to the easy question, and was shocked to find I had given him the wrong answer. I was new on the job, and I had done something terrible. I was a wet puppy as I sheepishly called him to tell him I had made a mistake. His response? "The only people what don't make mistakes are those what don't never do nothin'."

You can fault his grammar if you want to. But that would be a mistake. His grammar stood out as a blessing of kindness that I have carried with me more than fifty years. His words still ring in my ears today, as the Holy Spirit tells me the same thing when I go to the Lord confessing my mistakes. And He says, "Don't worry about the grammar, load the wagon full of love."

And that story has two lessons that you can look at this way: What to do when you mess up, and what you do when someone else messes up. When you mess up, you go to the Lord. You admit what you have done. And the two of you move on from there, with both of you lifted up. *That* is a good thing. And when someone else messes up? Remember Mr. Scott Hudgens, and the lesson on how a loving spirit responds to a wet puppy.

Try this. Think of something to thank God about. Thank God the Father, "in the name of the Lord Jesus Christ." Think of something else to thank Him about. Thank Him for it. Think of a third thing to thank Him about. Thank Him for it. Now, the first of those things you thanked Him for, if you thanked Him for it, that means He must have been somehow involved in it, right? So acknowledge His involvement. Praise Him for the fact He brought about the thing you thanked Him for, because not just anybody could do/would do what He did. He can so easily and so lovingly do things no one else can even start to do. Praise Him for it. Praise Him for His ability to do it, and praise Him for doing it for the good it provides, and the goodness it shows of Him. The same on the second thing you thanked Him for. The same on the third.

God wants you to talk to Him. He wants you to acknowledge Him and what He does in your life. And if you do that, if you spend that time with Him, that kind of time with Him, and if your praises are truth, He will inhabit your praises. You will get to know Him, better and better while learning to love Him, better and better. There is nothing better than that.

> Abide in Me, and I in you. As the branch cannot bear fruit of itself, unless it abides in the vine, neither can you, unless you abide in Me.
> I am the vine, you *are* the branches. He who abides in Me, and I in him, bears much fruit; for without Me you can do nothing (John 15:1-5).

Did you ever notice, while you were alone, you felt just fine, and a little while later, with no contact with anybody, you felt down? Nothing had happened, but you went from fine to down. Why would that be? It could be because you shifted from spiritually minded to carnally minded. Shift back. You can do that. Just flip the "minded" switch.

How? First, ask yourself if you want to be sad, or glad? Flipping the switch, or changing gears, is not possible unless you plan ahead. That means you plan your mind in advance. The problem is that if I slip fully into carnal-mindedness, it is then up to my carnal mind to get me out of being carnal minded. But my carnal mind will not do that. So I have to plan ahead.

What to do? While spiritual minded, use your mind to plan ahead. At the first appearance of a carnal minded trigger, plan to remember and say to yourself, "I will be sad about carnal mindedness, and I will be glad about spiritual mindedness." Then acknowledge God, thanking Him that He may have reminded you to do that.

The first carnal mind trigger is the key. Barney Fife had it right when he said, "Nip it in the bud!" Once fully accepted, the carnal-minded thought cannot so easily be dismissed, because carnal mindedness will not dismiss carnal mindedness. The *plan ahead* idea can work, as the spiritual mindedness of a prior moment can do the dismissing of the carnal mindedness of now. Remember "carnal brings sad, spiritual brings glad."

Everything Leads To Something Else.

"Every good and perfect gift is from above and cometh down from the Father" (James 1:17 KJV). Where do you think carnal-minded thoughts come from? Obviously not from God. Then where? Carnal minded thoughts seem so attractive, with pretty wrapping paper, a bow, and all that glitter. There once was a Trojan horse that was a gift. But what did that gift lead to for the ones who accepted it? It led to sad, not glad.

The quality of a gift is identified best by identifying the giver. It is the thought that counts. Trust the thought, and you will be trusting the giver of the thought. How can accepting a thought from Satan not lead to sad? Why do you think it will lead to glad?

Everything leads to something else, because it contains something else. It contains what it leads to next. What does carnal mindedness lead to? Carnal mindedness contains sin, so it leads to sin and the fruit of sin...sad, not glad.

What does spiritual mindedness generated from God's love lead to? Life - and glad. All the experiences of our whole life cry out that sin leads to sad, but following God's lead leads to glad. Choose glad. Yeah, you get to choose.

Be still. And listen.

Remember the old-fashioned preacher's quote about sin, "It's like if a bird flies over your head, that's not sin. But if you let it build a nest in your hair, that's sin." Likewise, if you have a sinful thought and ponder it, that leads to being carnal minded. Do not do it. When the thought flies to your head, recognize it as being a carnal thought and a threat to you and rather than letting it land, immediately think of the Lord Jesus Christ, and how much He loves you, and how much you love Him. Ponder that, and experience His presence and how good it is.

When I consider the importance of our choices, as described in Deuteronomy 30:15-20 as follows, I am so thankful that we serve a good, loving, omniscient God.

> See, I have set before you today life and good, death and evil, in that I command you today to love the LORD your God, to walk in His ways, and to keep His commandments, His statutes, and His judgments, that you may live and multiply; and the LORD your God will bless you in the land which you go to possess. But if your heart turns away so that you do not hear, and are drawn away, and worship other gods and serve them, I announce to you today that you shall surely perish; you shall not prolong *your* days in the land which you cross over the Jordan to go in and possess. I call heaven and earth as witnesses today against you, *that* I have set before you life and death, blessing and cursing; therefore choose life, that both you and your descendants may live; that you may love the LORD your God, that you may obey His voice, and that you may cling to Him, for He *is* your life and the length of your days; and that you may dwell in the land which the LORD swore to your fathers, to Abraham, Isaac, and Jacob, to give them.

The nature of God has not changed. The principles are the same today as then. Make the right choices and be glad, not sad.

When you love someone and they love you, telling each other about it is what you both want to do. Tell Him, and listen to Him tell you, "I love you. I love you so, so much!" Be still. And listen.

If you can't change gears? That is a problem.

If you lose control of your car - I mean your choices, your free will, your life - if you lose control and can't change gears, that is a problem. The sin that you chose to follow, now has possession of your freedom, your God-given free will has been hi-jacked. And your identity as a child of God has been stolen. You don't have it anymore, not if you can't change gears you don't. Whatever happened to "I can do all things through Christ who strengthens me" (Philippians 4:13)? You pushed it into a closet when you let your identity be stolen. Without your identity, you are without your power. You are still saved, but you are living the life of a caterpillar, a worm, instead of a beautiful butterfly. Even more, you should be soaring on wings of eagles, but if you can't put it in reverse, if you can't back up and turn around and go in the other direction, you are no longer driving, you are being driven. And there is nothing you can do about it. You are trapped. There is nothing you can do about it. Except, thank goodness, there is, if you are willing to seek help.

There is help if you admit to yourself you need the help. If you think you can wait and work it out yourself, after just one more time, you lose. You will continue to be driven, not led by the Lord, but driven by sin. Even in your present condition, you know that is true, and you know not only that you cannot change gears, you know that without help you still won't be able to change gears tomorrow. So admit it.

Where to find help? Yogi Berra said, "You can see a lot just by looking." Seek the help, and you can find it. With the Internet available, you can find help just by looking. Pray about it. Pray about finding the right help. If your family is depending on you, that can be the most important prayer you ever prayed.

You say you have tried so hard, so often, and failed? So you don't try anymore? You give up? Why? Don't you know you have the power of Christ in you? Maybe you haven't driven your car in a while, and the battery is dead and the car really looks dirty. What to do? You get some jumper cables, you get a boost and you recharge the battery. You clean up the car. When you get that car of yours in good running condition, you have no doubt that it has the power to do what you need it to do. That is what it was made for. Of course it has the power. You need some help

from someone who has jumper cables to recharge your battery, your

spiritual battery. But with a little help, you can come to live in Christ, and

in Him there is no way you will not have the power to do what He calls

you to do. You can do it, because He can do it through you if you will just

acknowledge His call. Proverbs 3:5, 6 is the stock number of some good

jumper cables.

You still say you know you cannot break the habit, or the

addiction, or overcome the boredom without it? That is absolutely not

true. You can. And the boredom is a false picture painted, perpetrated by

the carnal mind. You just need a little help. And you are just the one to

give it to you. No one else can do it for you. Others can tell you how, but

you have to do it, all by yourself, with Christ cheering for you. Very

importantly, you have to do it *before* you are in a carnal mind. How? By

planning your mind in advance, anticipating what you will do the *instant*

your gear shifts to carnal mindedness.

The instant of the shift to carnal mindedness will seem like just a

little thing. But oh, it is about the biggest thing that can ever befall a man.

Speaking of "fallen man," that was exactly what tripped up Adam. I

mean, what harm can there be in such a thing as taking a piece of fruit from a tree, right? That is a magnificent example of what still happens to man today. It always starts with such a little thing. And that is exactly why man must take Barney Fife's advice, and "nip it in the bud."

The serpent said to Eve, "Has God said you will surely die? You will not surely die." Yeah, go ahead, taking the fruit is such a little thing. Only all of mankind will fall because of it. So what to do? Plan your mind ahead of time.

Just had a carnal thought? Do not ignore it. If you just ignore it, it will lead to another. But also do not give it the time of day. Just call it what it is. Say to yourself, "That's a carnal thought." *Then* you can address the reasons you choose to go somewhere else in your mind. You trust God to provide the good you need, not the author of carnal thoughts. Next, talk with Him. Trust His omniscience and His love to know and to give you what you will look back on and thank Him for. Call the carnal thought what it is. "Carnal thought!" It is nothing more than a carnal thought, and you do not want to abide that. You do not need to dwell on the content of the carnal thought. That substance is not important. The point is it is a carnal thought and you called it out.

The author of carnal thoughts doesn't want you to call it what it is. He wants to fly in under the radar. He wants that carnal thought to lead to the next, without your realizing the process has begun. Truth. Call a spade a spade and a carnal thought a carnal thought. That is the spiritually-minded thing to do, and the gear is shifted, without your struggling to shift gears. All you did was announce the truth. Another victory. So call a victory a victory and give your spirit the congratulations it deserves. And your soul will be blessed again.

Sometimes you might say, "That was not a carnal thought, but it was almost a carnal thought, and I stopped it in its tracks." Take credit, another victory.

What the carnal thought is about is not relevant. The enemy is a carnal thought. Call it by its name, a carnal thought, truth prevails - and truth is an open door to spiritual mindedness. The switch is flipped. It is not about what you want. It is about appreciating what God has given you. He has given you Himself. He is the giver of true life. Goliath could not intimidate David. The "giants" in the Promised Land could not intimidate Caleb. And you should not let the giants of carnal mindedness intimidate you. You can do what God says do. Stop digging the hole you are in. Walk with God and win.

Habits can be broken in three days.
Addictions can take a little longer;
But every day you walk with God
Is a day you get a little stronger.

124

Jesus said in John 16:33, "These things I have spoken to you, that in Me you may have peace. In the world you will have tribulation; but be of good cheer, I have overcome the world."

And yet in Romans 7:19-20, Paul said, "For the good that I will to do, I do not do; but the evil I will not to do, that I practice. Now if I do what I will not to do, it is no longer I who do it, but sin that dwells in me." How did that work out for Paul? Well, it was about five years later that Paul wrote, "I can do all things through Christ, Who strengthens me" (Philippians 4:13). So did that indicate Paul 'somehow' overcame the sin in him? I don't know, but I do know Paul also wrote, "Pray without ceasing." So you know what I think? I think Paul prayed all the way to Carnegie Hall, and Jesus walked with him every step of the way.

What if you practice, practice, practice trying to pray without ceasing, and you fail? Are you better off or worse off for trying? What if you practice, practice, practice trying to pray without ceasing, and you succeed? Are you better off or worse off for having tried? What if the answer to both questions is the same? What if the answer is as plain as the nose on your face? What if God loves you a lotta bit? Right now. Right this minute. What if you realize He loves you so much, that you just can't hardly stand it. What if His love for you is as plain as the nose on your face?

Let him who has ears to hear, hear. And let him who has a nose on his face, seek the face of God.

Praise to God brings God's presence "to mind," and when God really shows up in the mind Satan has to get out of Dodge.

The biggest and real battlegrounds in this world are inside a person's mind and heart. But you can always praise God at least silently, so you can always bring to mind God's presence. Does it take practice? Yes, but that is how you get to Carnegie Hall. That is how you ultimately achieve the goal of walking with God rather than running from Him. Life or death - choose life. For more information on what that choice is about, start with John 10:10 a few paragraphs from here, and the subsequent discussion.

The last verse of the last Psalm says: "Let every thing that hath breath praise the LORD. Praise ye the LORD" (KJV).

Let me give you a clue. Praising God is for your benefit, not God's. He would get along just fine without your praise, from your little mouth. Except He loves you and wants what is best for you. He created us in such a way that if we will appreciate the truly good of the world, our appreciation will bless us. God is the 'Goodest' and God is Spirit. If you choose instead to feed your carnal mind with what amounts to praise for carnal objects rather than feed your spiritual mind with the unfathomable truth of His love, wisdom, omnipotence, omnipresence, glory, and goodness, then you will miss out on good He has for you.

Carnal-minded thoughts give undue attention to carnal objects. The carnal mind is fed with such activity, then seeks its own pleasure from it, and therefore is motivated not to change. But the mind of a Christian must change. Even if you think you wouldn't mind being double-minded, the Holy Spirit will make life miserable for the double-minded Christian just as we make His life miserable inside us. As necessity is the mother of invention, so necessity is the greatest motivator of change.

Truth: The Lamb is worthy of all praise. I think one reason praise is such a powerful weapon in a Christian's arsenal is that it puts into words the ultimate Truth about Jesus. *When the mind and heart are joined in spirit and in truth in love for the Lord, nothing can have more power, and nothing can conquer that union.*

Undue attention to carnal objects gives implied tribute of praise to a false god of carnality. When God provides something that we like, it is natural for us to want more. And more. And more. Whether we see a pretty flower, a pretty woman, or a pretty lot of money that God has blessed us to see, we must learn to appreciate what He has given us, and not let a carnal mind insist on dwelling on an unauthorized "more." That kind of obsessive wanting becomes lust, which is not authorized by God. He has even better things for us, but our lust stops His blessings from flowing to us. To receive His blessings and not His slow-but-sure punishment, we *must* learn to change gears at the first inkling of carnal-mindedness.

God loves us regardless. But when a child needs motivation to change his bad conduct, and love and words don't solve the matter, the parent has to resort to more drastic measures. God invented powerful parenting, and if you can't use oil to change those gears, you may be in for a drastic overhaul. And they cost a lot.

Above all, remember to plan your mind. Plan how you will react at the first instance of a carnal thought. Of course carnal thoughts will still come, but with help and proper planning and a determination to free yourself from sleeping in wet urine grass - the grass that looks greener on the other side of the fence - you will learn to react properly at the first instance of a carnal thought. The success will give you a victorious walk that only you will understand and that you will know is a sweet taste

of the life that Jesus was describing when He said, "I have come that they

may have life, and that they may have it more abundantly" (John 10:10).

The Devil, the flesh and the world promise such a life. But the

Devil is the father of all lies, and so easily blinds us to the better life God

really has for us. You trusted Jesus with your salvation? Now trust Him

with how to live. At the first instance, turn and go in the opposite

direction from the urine grass on the other side of the fence. Whew!

Through the grace of my Lord and savior Jesus Christ, I walk with

God. He is my father. I want to acknowledge Him in every way. I need

Him to direct...

    my feet
    my thoughts
    my words
    my actions
    my passion
    my quietness.

The flesh wants to chase rabbits; the spirit needs to put up barriers

in advance, and to award rewards for instant changing of gears. Claim

frequent victories and enjoy the claiming.

At the first hint of carnal thought, replace it with something like,

"Glory to God in the highest," and "The Lamb is worthy. Glory to God in

the highest." Claim that as a victory. But it is just a start. The carnal minded activity is held dear by the flesh, but is an abomination to your spirit in Christ. Your spirit in Christ must win, and sooner-rather-than-later would make life easier on both the flesh and the spirit. And the winner would be your soul. Dumb flesh. Beautiful spirit. Beautiful Spirit!

Plan your reaction. Be mentally prepared. When temptation comes, and it will come, pull out a song from the past. Plan ahead, and your soul will be blessed.

When you sing that song, remember the greatest commandment, remember your love is true, and it is due, because He first loved you.

You can do it. You can walk the line. And love it. All else pales in comparison.

Our souls are NOT born again! Our spirits are.

People can get confused about the distinction between their souls and their spirits. In addressing that, look how Hebrews 4:12 KJV is true in its claim about the Word of God.

> For the word of God is quick, and powerful, and sharper than any two-edged sword, *piercing even to the dividing asunder of soul and spirit*, and of the joints and marrow, and is a discerner of the thoughts and intents of the heart.

The Bible's clarity on this subject seems to me to be unquestionable. Our spirits are born of incorruptible seed when we accept Jesus, but our souls (minds, emotions, etc.) still need to be *purified*, that is, cleansed:

> Seeing ye have *purified your souls* in obeying the truth through the Spirit unto unfeigned love of the brethren, see that ye love one another with a pure heart fervently: *Being born again,* not of corruptible seed, but of incorruptible, by the word of God, which liveth and abideth forever (1 Peter 1:22-23 KJV).

Our spirit is reborn and instantly made new when we accept Christ, but the soul is not born again. Our souls are transformed by the renewing of our minds:

> And be not conformed to this world: but *be ye transformed by the renewing of your mind,* that ye may prove what is that good, and acceptable, and perfect, will of God (Romans 12:2 KJV).

Scripture tells us our spirit is born again, and after that our soul is purified/sanctified by the renewing of our mind. Spirit and soul clearly are not the same thing. The description in 1 Thessalonians 5:23 KJV is:

> And the very God of peace sanctify you wholly; and I pray God your whole spirit *and* soul and body be preserved blameless unto the coming of our Lord Jesus Christ.

Addiction Fiction:

Is addiction fiction? More accurately, it will be history in the future. Since our bodies are only temporary, in that sense addiction now is history in the future. There are many kinds of addiction. We think it is all about chemicals. But it is not. We live in a physical world, but it is also, and even more so, a spiritual world. The physical part is temporary for us, the physical world is a learning center for us, for our soul, which belongs to our spirit. The spiritual, the part we cannot see with our eyes, is the real world, or rather our real existence. For every physical action, there is a spiritual action at the root. When you become addicted to something, you learn it is your Kryptonite. Superman became helpless when exposed to Kryptonite. Yeah, I know, he is fiction. But so is addiction, in a cause and effect sense, because addiction comes through the body, and the body is temporary, but the addiction can affect the eternal spirit and soul of the addiction victim and those he comes in contact with. The origin of the addiction is in the spiritual world which triggered the addiction

Anyway, addiction is a trap, like Kryptonite, and the best way to avoid it is to stay away from it. If you are already trapped, it is not the end of the world. Walk with God. Talk with God. Study His Holy Word. Love Him, love your brother as yourself, listen to Him, listen to Him, and listen to Him. He, and you, and Romans 8:28 will prevail. It may seem like a lost cause. It is not. I had a dream. While I was asleep, someone named Christopher said to me, "You had a problem." The word "had" is past tense. I woke up. I did still have a problem. I learned that the very next day. But Christopher used the word "had," past tense. God sees the future, and in the present He speaks in the future of the past which is yet to come. I knew my problem would be in the past in the future. That was encouragement enough for me.

You don't have to have a dream to survive Kryptonite. God works with each of us in a special way designed just for us. Walk with God, and thereby keep Kryptonite at a safe distance, far away. He loves you, and wants to protect you. And sometimes, He is the only one who can. The only one who will. The only one who can raise you up. The only one who loves you enough to give you His all, when the only thing that can help is His all, in His love. "With God nothing is impossible." It may take awhile. It may take a long time. It may only take a day. But with God, you have all the time in the world and then some, if you walk with God. You can be as close to God as you want. It is your move.

Spiritual Mindedness Trumps Hard Times

Once I have a glorified body rather than this physical body, I will be only spiritually minded and never carnally minded. A carnal mind without a carnal body would be useless. We already know a carnal mind with a carnal body is a foolish mind. On earth, we get to grow and develop our spiritual mindedness. Perhaps it would be more accurate to say we get to let Him grow, in us, and develop our spiritual mindedness.

My hard times lead me to seek the Lord, which leads to development of spiritual mindedness. If I would work on spiritual mindedness before the hard times, likely the hard times would not be so needed in my development. It is better to accept that you cannot have something, and walk on solid ground, than to sink in quicksand trying to grasp it anyway.

The Holy Spirit is not here just to give us comfort. He wants to guide us, and it is up to us to be open to that guidance. Without openness to Him, we revert to guidance the hard way. With openness to Him, we become more like Jesus. You become like what you focus on most.

We saw Peter exposed to that lesson when he walked on water. He began to sink when he changed his focus from Jesus to the storm.

The saying, "Don't tell God how big the storm is, tell the storm how big God is," may sound trite, but try it. The reason Peter was able to walk on water in the first place was because he asked Jesus to tell him to. When Jesus did that - the result was a miracle. Miracles, large and small, happen when we do what God says do - keep our eyes on Him.

I suspect that the more spiritual minded a person becomes, the more force Satan wants to bring against the person. Therefore consistency becomes important. Walking with the Lord provides some protection against attacks. Dropping back to carnal mindedness, makes one more vulnerable than before, because greater evil forces are ready to take advantage of the slip.

Still, if one survives, he or she becomes stronger than ever. Fighting battles, and surviving, makes us stronger from the exercise. Of course, unnecessarily creating a need to fight battles would be dangerously unwise.

The greater calling is to walk with the Lord without ceasing. To walk with the Lord with joy. To walk with the Lord in the fullness of His love. To walk with the Lord with an ever-growing awareness of His presence. He wants us to walk with Him. He tells us to. So yes, the greater calling is to walk with the Lord without ceasing, in joy, in the fullness of His love, with an ever-growing awareness of His presence. It starts with His love, loving Him, and obedience to His infinite wisdom. That walk is a taste of heaven, and the glory of that feast will never end.

Long about now, you would need to thank the Lord for His presence, remembering the fact that He inhabits the praise of His people. You should be able to take it from there.

> Abide in Me, and I in you. As the branch cannot bear fruit of itself, unless it abides in the vine, neither can you, unless you abide in Me.
> I am the vine, you *are* the branches. He who abides in Me, and I in him, bears much fruit; for without Me you can do nothing (John 15:1-5).

The Sting

Remember the movie "The Sting?" It was not a spiritual movie, but spiritual principles can be found in many films and stories.

Have you ever thought about the sting operation God pulled on the devil? He allowed evil to take 100% innocent Jesus the Christ and kill him. Yet, with Jesus rising then from the dead, we can see Jesus conquered death and brought from that most evil act, the culmination of the singular most important result in the history of the world. How would you like to work with Jesus on a similar sting operation, on a smaller scale, of course, with no pain, just gain?

At the first inkling of a carnal thought, thank God, in spirit and in truth, and praise His omniscience, and omnipotence, for allowing such a thing as a carnal thought to happen - I didn't say ask Him to allow more carnal thoughts - just thank Him for that one. Remember that the type of carnal thought is irrelevant. It is just up to you to call it what it is, a carnal thought. Thank Him for using that thought for a good purpose, to trigger you to remember to pray without ceasing. Use it for that. Praise Him for His love and for His goodness, His omniscience and His omnipresence, and then see if His overwhelming presence will just blow away that pitiful, icky, inkling of a carnal thought.

Remember that in football when you are overmatched, the way to topple a big powerful ball carrier is to hit him near the ankles and let his own weight bring him down? Remember David slew Goliath with a stone to the unarmored space right between the eyes? What *spiritual* offensive weapon like a slingshot can hit carnal thoughts at the ankles, or right between the eyes? The slingshot, the offensive weapon, is love. The ammunition, the stone, is praise to God. When you praise the Creator, in spirit and in truth - it has to be in spirit and in truth - with practice, the knowledge of His presence topples the overpowering allure of the carnal desire.

Thank the Lord that the carnal thought gives you a needed reminder to pray. Praise Him for the wisdom of that, for the goodness that can be found in that as a sting. When Satan sends you a thought that draws you closer to the Lord, it is the last thing he wants to do. So why wouldn't your action of praising the Lord the instant it arrives motivate him to stop sending such things? Practice, and praise the Lord for letting the truth set you free, since, "You had (past tense, in the future) a problem."

A word to the wise is sufficient. But most of us need a whole lot more. More than wise, God is omniscient, and the Bible has every good principle that we need. Yet we still need help in sorting out and applying the principles. The Holy Spirit is here to guide us in that. That part would be too voluminous for books. John 21:25 KJV: "And there are also many other things which Jesus did, the which, if they should be written every one, I suppose that even the world itself could not contain the books that should be written. Amen."

Moses followed the cloud by day and the fire by night. Walk with God. He's got your back.

"But Coach, I don't have a history of praising God."
"But Coach, I don't have a history of trying to pray without ceasing."
"But Coach, I don't have a history of following..."

A paradigm is not two dimes. And human beings are not bodies that have a spirit and a soul. We are spiritual beings that have a soul and a temporary body. The body is just the garden in which the spirit lives and its soul grows.

The spirit is contained in the pre-born baby's body, in the womb. With exceptions like the episode described in Luke 1:44, being contained seems strange to the spirit, and a new paradigm begins, as its soul blossoms in containment with it, creating ability and motivation - to learn and to make choices. The Luke 1:44 episode, when John the Baptist jumped for joy in the womb, was where He spiritually discerned Jesus entering the house in Mary's womb. That identification of joy in a pre-born baby may be unprecedented. Sadly, the courts do not seem to grasp. John the Baptist was a human being while he was still in the womb. Somebody ought to tell them.

Once our spirit is born again, it is able to lead the soul in the transformation described in Romans 12:2 KJV. The spirit and the soul meld together as the soul grows. The unbridled power of the spirit becomes influenced by its soul, and the soul draws power from its spirit. And the temporary earthly body is yet a temporary garden for that process.

Psalm 139:13 (HCSB) says, "For it was You who created my inward parts; You knit me together in my mother's womb." I suspect that verse refers as much to the knitting together of the spirit and the soul, as knitting together the physical aspects of the body. The knitting together of the spirit and the soul in the body, suggests a great need for direct spiritual attention, and God is Spirit.

The Bible tells us that when we graduate, we will receive a new, glorified body. So for now, see yourself for what you are. You are God's workmanship, and He is growing you, whether you are still in the womb, while your mother is reading this to you, or whether you are seventy-five years old, or even older than that. God is still growing your soul, which has influence over your spirit, in your temporary body as the spirit and the soul become one, in harmony.

Closing thought: We truly are fearfully and wonderfully made. In my mind I can hear Kris Kristofferson singing "Why Me Lord?" and the words are still true. It is only after God kneads us that we realize how we need Him. No, we don't just happen. We are God's workmanship.

Chapter 10:
It's a Jungle Out There

Life on earth is a song in the midst of spiritual warfare, and carnal minds can't win in spiritual warfare. "For to be carnally minded is death, but to be spiritually minded is life and peace." Romans 8:6. Therefore, not being conscious of God nor loving God as we should is death. Being conscious of God and loving God as we should, is life and peace.

Shakespeare's Hamlet didn't exactly say it right. He was seeking a noble course, but "To be or not to be" is not the question. We already are. And we always will be. The question is to be carnally minded or to be spiritually minded. And God answered that unmistakably in Deuteronomy 30:15-17 KJV, saying, "See, I have set before thee this day life and good, and death and evil; in that I command thee this day to Love the Lord thy God...and the Lord thy God shall bless thee...But if thine heart turn away, so that thou wilt not hear...."

When Abraham obediently placed his son on the altar, to give up his son to die for the Lord, he wasn't being carnally minded, he was being spiritually minded. The result was not death, but life and peace. Though David's life was a marathon of spiritual battles, and though he went through a period of being carnally minded, he started strong and finished strong, and was certainly not being carnally minded when he wrote

Psalm 105:1-5:

> Oh, give thanks to the LORD!
> Call upon His name;
> Make known His deeds among the peoples!
> Sing to Him, sing psalms to Him;
> Talk of all His wondrous works!
> Glory in His holy name;
> Let the hearts of those rejoice who seek the LORD!
> Seek the LORD and His strength;
> Seek His face evermore!
> Remember His marvelous works which He has done,
> His wonders, and the judgments of His mouth,

Oh Father! Sometimes I *feel* as if I don't even know how to love. You are so worthy. But I *feel* so inadequate, so inadequate in my love for you. You deserve all my love, but I *feel* I don't know how to love. Oh Father! Sometimes I try to draw on my *faith* to tell me I love You deeply. You are so worthy. I don't know how You could be so good as to send Jesus to die for us. And yet You did. And yet my faith is inadequate. I still question the depth of my love for you. You deserve all my love. The Lord Jesus Christ deserves all my love. Yet my *faith feels* inadequate.

Father, it is a *fact* that I love You. Lord Jesus, it is a *fact* that I love You. Holy Spirit, it is a *fact* that I love You. I know not what the future holds, but this moment, with tears coming down my cheeks and my nose running, I love you with all my heart, all my soul, all my strength, all my might, all my mind.

Feelings ebb and flow. Even *faith* ebbs and flows. But Your love for me is a *fact*, and my love for You is a *fact*, and Love endures *forever*!

> For I am persuaded that neither death nor life, nor angels nor principalities nor powers, nor things present nor things to come, nor height nor depth, nor any other created thing, shall be able to separate us from the love of God which is in Christ Jesus our Lord. Romans 8:38-39.

Sometimes when we sin, we might think God is mad at us so we just compartmentalize Him, closing Him off from our awareness of Him. So we don't talk to Him. But that's the *opposite* of God's desire. The *Opposite!* Frank Daniels said, "God wants us to talk to Him." God asked Moses, "What's that in your hand?" Moses said, "A rod." But God already knew the answer. So why did he ask Moses?

Remember, God asked Ezekiel, "Son of man, can these bones live?" Ezekiel said, "O Lord God, You know." But God already knew what Ezekiel's answer would be. So why did He ask Ezekiel?

God wants us to talk to Him, even, no, especially when we have sinned. If we have accepted Jesus, then when God looks at us, He sees

Jesus. And He wants us to talk and get things right with Him. He doesn't want un-confessed sin (which He already knows about anyway) to come between us and Him.

The next chapter of this book is titled, "Isaiah 43:7". But before you go there, please open your Bible and read Luke 7:43. In fact, read verses 39-43.

You will see that Luke 7:43 is a very personal note from God to you, with His telling *how much you love Him*. He also tells me right there in His Holy Word how much I love Him, and it is a different amount! So, if you would, just go read those five verses. And now would be a good time. 43:7 will be happy to yield to 7:43 for a while.

There will be an intermission.

While we wait, for those who do not have a Bible, you can be reading the following pages, Robyn's tenth grade homework for English class at Tucker High School. It's the story of a man named Avery Goodman.

Robyn Ivey

Period 2

3-10-00

Despite his wealth, Avery Goodman was very poor. He always thought he needed more and more. The more he had, the more he thought he needed. It was really a matter of whom he needed. Sure, he had many friends, but none liked him for who he was, just for what he had. He was always angry. He was angry at his father, angry at his so-called friends, and angry at himself He felt something was missing in his life.

Avery was a prisoner of prosperity and a sponge of greed. He wasted much of his wealth on gadgets he thought would make him happy. Bullying poorer kids gave him passing pleasure, but he still was not convinced of his own superiority. He felt empty inside.

His father traveled around the world on business trips, leaving Avery alone in his luxurious mansion with his servants. He loved and hated his father for the riches and for always being gone. Every once in a while, Avery would receive letters from his father. But his father's recent letters were different. They conveyed a sense of love and joy. Avery thought that this love and joy was what could fill the hole in his heart. His father seemed to be a more complete man. Avery wanted whatever it was that made his father so happy.

Every year, Avery's father came home for Christmas. This Christmas season started the same as all the others, but it transformed him forever. Avery was at the airport to meet his father. All of a sudden, he heard people screaming. He followed the crowd and saw an airplane in flames after it had exploded. A horrible thought gripped Avery. "Daddy!" he cried. He ran as close to the flames as he could, but there was no hope of any survivors. Avery had to back away from the flames. He knelt and then lay flat on the ground and started crying out to the God he had never before acknowledged. After a while, he arose and walked back to the air terminal.

"Avery!" he heard from a voice in the distance. Startled, he turned and could not believe his eyes. "What's all the commotion? What happened?" his father asked. Avery froze. It was a ghost? It was Daddy! "Daddy, you're okay!" Avery exclaimed as he rushed to him and threw his arms around him. "Yes, I'm okay," his dad replied. "But, why didn't you meet me at gate G like you were supposed to? What's happened?" Avery told his dad everything, that he thought his father was dead, and that in despair he had even cried out to God.

His dad gave him a hug and told him to come sit down and talk. His dad explained, "I have been praying for you to come to accept Jesus as your Savior as I did a few months ago. It has completely changed my life and I am a new man inside."

Avery responded, "I know, Dad. I can see a change in you, just as I read in your letters. What does it mean to 'accept Jesus as your Savior'?"

"Avery, I didn't know the answer to that question just a few months ago. It all started for me with a Gideons Bible in a hotel room. I've studied and I've studied and I've studied. What I've learned is this: By nature, man's heart runs from God and rebels against Him. The Bible calls this 'sin'. Romans 3:23, says, 'For all have sinned and come short of the glory of God.' Yet God loves you and wants to save you from sin, to offer you a new life of hope. John 10:10 says, 'I am come that they might have life, and that they might have it more abundantly.' To give you this gift of salvation, God made a way through His Son, Jesus Christ. Romans 5:8 says, 'But God commendeth his love toward us, in that, while we were yet sinners, Christ died for us.' You receive this gift by faith alone. Ephesians 2:8-9, says, 'For it is by grace you have been saved, through faith – and this is not from yourselves, it is the gift of God – not by works, so that no one can boast.'"

Avery said, "I've never thought about all this before. I'm amazed that you know all these things. Somehow I feel ready to learn about this faith. I'm so relieved that you're alive and here to talk with me like this."

"Avery, I apologize for not being here for you most of your life. Only now do I realize how much I love you. I always loved you, but I just didn't realize how much. The most important thing in my life now is hearing you say that you feel ready to learn about this faith."

"How does one accept God's gift of faith?"

"Faith is a decision of your heart demonstrated by genuine repentance and changed actions in your life. Romans 10:9, says that if you confess with your mouth, 'Jesus is Lord,' and believe in your heart that God raised him from the dead, you will be saved."

His father said, "Avery, it would be the best Christmas present I ever had if you could tell me that you are ready right now to believe Jesus died for your sins and to receive new life through him."

"Dad, I'm ready. Just tell me what to do."

His dad said, "Then pray after me, 'Dear God, I know I'm a sinner. I believe Jesus died to forgive me of my sins. I now accept Your offer of eternal life. Thank You for forgiving me of all my sin. Thank You for my new life. From this day forward, I will choose to follow You."

Avery prayed each sentence after his dad. At that moment, he could feel the renewal of his heart. The hole in his heart was finally filled with the joy of his salvation in Christ.

Chapter 11:

Isaiah 43:7

Isaiah 43:7 KJV, says, "...I have created him for my glory..."

I am reminded of the time when Robyn was 26 months old and she was in the bathroom watching me shave. She said, "You want to hear a song I just wrote?" I said "Yes!" She sang it. It was a really cute little song - only five words, which she repeated over and over to a catchy original tune as she slapped her knees in rhythm. I was surprised and delighted. But I was more surprised at what she did when she finished. She closed her eyes and lowered her head and said, "God, thank You for giving me that song. Amen." Glory to God for that!

The medical assistant at Georgia Cancer Specialists was attaching my chemotherapy I.V. bag. I asked her how long she had been doing this kind of work. I think she said fifteen years. I said, "You must have helped a mighty lot of people in so many years." She replied, "I just thank the Lord He gave me the opportunity and the wisdom to do it."

I had not previously noticed she had wisdom. She had great wisdom. She had automatically, without pause, deflected all praise and glory away from herself and to the Lord. That's where it belongs. God

---

appreciates being acknowledged, in spirit and in truth, as He *is* Spirit and Truth. If you don't want His blessings, just don't acknowledge them. And like people do when they are ignored, the blessings will just go away. Of course we all want the blessings, sometimes we are just a little lazy, having souls that are inertia prone, and we don't remember to acknowledge Him and what He does in our lives. If a word to the wise is sufficient, the word is "acknowledge."

Yes, God created us for His glory! But why? Why did God create us for His glory? Why didn't He just do something else for His glory?

I think we first need to look at why creating us would bring Him glory. God is love, and even though no one else but God had the ability to fully create us in His image, He didn't just create us. He created us with loving care, and nurtured us. Why? He is still growing us. Why? He created us with the ability to turn away from Him, or to love Him and have fellowship with Him. Why? He created us in His own image, which is to His glory, and our good. But why didn't He just create us as the most super computers that will ever exist, with no free will? Yes, He is worthy of all our praise. And that is glorious. But why did He create us

for His glory, rather than just doing something else for His glory?
Again the answer is love.

Jeremiah 1:5 says, "Before I formed you in the womb I knew
you...." And He loved you. He created you for His glory, but He did that
for His glory *because* He loved you. And He created me for His glory
because He loved me. God can do anything He wants to do for whatever
reason He wants to, and the result of whatever God does is glorious and to
His glory. But He chose to create us for His glory *because* He loved us.
And He proved His love at Calvary. On the Cross. Knowing all that, how
can we not love Him with all our heart, all our soul, all our strength, all
our might, all our mind. He is the One who gave me my heart, my soul,
my strength, my might, my mind. And my salvation. How can I not give
Him my heart and everything else.

The Greatest Commandment doesn't command me to do anything
for God that He hasn't already done for me. God first loved me, with all
God's everything! 100% unconditional love. And that is more than a lotta
bit. How many people don't even know there *is* a "Greatest
Commandment?" Someone should tell them.

150

The Purpose of Love

To the Lord, I respectfully say with thanksgiving and praise, to borrow a perspective from my brother, Bob, as he spoke in his last months here on earth:

> The goblet used by Jesus at the last supper did not have a great capacity, but its purpose was glorious, for it touched the lips of God! You have taught me the value of something can be known only by knowing its purpose, not its capacity.
>
> Sometimes a thing's purpose can be found only by asking, "What did it do?" In my mind and heart, just writing this book was priceless to me in awakening my love for You, Lord, and all people. I give You all the praise and all the glory for that. Sometimes a thing has multiple purposes. If just one reader receives just one blessing from this book that will be a wonderful bonus. To this book I say, "I am praying for you. I pray that you be a goblet full and running over for your readers, far beyond our capacity."

Chapter 12:

The Classics

My Fondest Memories list includes my two oldest sons and me. Some with them - Bill and Dallas - so young that we pretended they were one football team and I was the other, and it became a level playing field because I was allowed to run only on my knees, so they scored a lot.

The greatest memory with them (other than their births) was when they were just a little older, and we checked into a motel so we could go swimming and then have room service as we watched the Georgia/Florida game on television. Georgia was down by 1 with 90 seconds left, and almost zero hope, 92 yards away from the goal. Bill and Dallas were jumping up and down for joy, on the bed (don't tell anybody I said that, it just all of a sudden happened) as Lindsey Scott caught the ball and I was yelling, "He's gonna score! He's gonna score! He's gonna score!" and Lindsey Scott was running down the field, 92 yards with time running out, giving the Georgia Bulldogs their greatest victory ever, on the way to the national championship. Lord thank you for Dallas and Bill (and Lindsey Scott), and the memories. Nice coincidence that the only time we

152

ever rented a motel room to watch a football game, it was the greatest game in Georgia's history! WOW! (See John 21:25).

Can you say the Lord would or would not be involved in the outcome of the game? I acknowledge He well could have been. It may be more likely that He simply saw what the outcome would be, and therefore led us to rent the motel room. Proverbs 3:5, 6 is surely a good thing to work on. Go Dawgs!

Bill and Dallas each earned a bachelor's degree from the University of Georgia. Then Bill earned a degree at Medical College of Georgia to become a physical therapist. After that he went to Georgia State University and earned a double master's in medical business administration. Dallas earned a master's in economics at Georgia State University, then a law degree at Mercer University. They got their smarts from their mother, who had graduated summa cum laude from the University of Georgia.

I know God has a sweet tooth, because when He made Bill and Dallas' mother, Dale Miller, He dumped in all the sweetness He could find. Then He went out and found some more. And He put that in too. Lord, thank You for Dale.

Because of Dale, Bill and Dallas turned out to be fine family men, loving husbands and fathers. The fact that their step-dad, Louis Miller, was a Methodist minister probably helped more than a little bit too. God is so good.

Bill and Dallas' maternal granddaddy, Dallas Mobley, was a retired F.B.I. agent. He was also Vince Dooley's biggest fan. Vince Dooley was the coach of many great Georgia football teams. I was Dooley's second biggest fan. Today, I'm Mark Richt's biggest fan. Shortly after Richt became the head football coach at the University of Georgia, he kind of got a lock on my heart when, right after a big victory, on national television, he gave thanks to the Lord Jesus Christ. I think he will be in God's Hall of Fame.

My granddaddy was the secretary of his church, Camp Creek Primitive Baptist Church. His granddaddy was the secretary of his church. I suppose his church might have been Ivey Baptist Church in Ivey, Georgia. His name was Charles Ivey, and I traveled to Ivey, Georgia once, years ago. I saw the Ivey city limits sign, Ivey Georgia on the water tank, Ivey Feed and Seed Store, and Ivey Baptist Church. And some houses. I believe there were some other stores, but seeing so much "Ivey" sort of clouded my vision, and my limited-to-begin-with memory may be fading.

Charles Ivey founded Ivey, Georgia, but based on Jesus' words to the Pharisees, about God being able to raise up descendants of Abraham from rocks, I might should point out to my grandchildren that we might should be careful about being proud of being anyone's descendants. And yet I am very adequately pleased with my ancestors, and I hope they will be able to say the same about their descendants.

My daddy didn't start to school until he was seven years old, because they lived out in the country. His mother thought six years old was too young for him to walk several miles twice a day. But still he graduated from high school a few days after he became 16, and received a master's degree from Auburn (then Alabama Polytechnic Institute) at a young age.

We didn't have criminals in our family. My hat is off to the folks who let God's love lift them out of such a heritage, to begin a new chain of love for their children to carry forward. They are real heroes, and I would want to give them any encouragement possible. How hard such a heritage would be. But how glorious would be the success. If you have done that, God bless you - even more than He has already.

"Have you lived in Georgia all your life?" *I hope not!* The first time I heard that joke, I knew it would be a classic. I may still be the only one that knows it. But it is a classic to me. To me, that means that in my opinion it is of the first or highest quality or class or rank. One reason the classics are the best is because over time we have the opportunity to let our love grow for the ones we consider special. Another reason they are the best is they really are the best!

Here is another classic. My opinion, of course. "Can you tell me how to get to Stone Mountain from here?" *No, you can't get there from here. First you have to go to the second traffic light, turn right, and....*

Life can be confusing, and you can't get to heaven from here. Jesus said first you have to be born again. And some of us don't follow directions very well. God can compensate for our confusion. He can make adjustments, if we let Him, but we do have to be born again. He will never love you any more, or any less, than He does right now. 100%. I think it is time we returned the favor.

Fatherly Moments:

My daddy's name was Julian C. Ivey. As a small boy I delighted

that he and Jesus Christ had the same initials. *I still think it's cool.* I also

loved his humorous dry wit. One day I drove him to his monthly

appointment at Dr. Byrd's office.

Dr. Bird: Do you have any memory problems?
J.C. Ivey: Well, no, unless you would count the therefore problem?
Dr. Bird: The "therefore problem?"
J.C. Ivey: Yeah. Sometimes I get up and go in another room, and then it
is hard to remember what I came in there for!

I took him to visit the eye surgeon:
Dr. McManus: Can you read the top line?
J.C. Ivey: Naw. I can see it fine, but I can't quite make out what it says.
It's in some sort of foreign language!

At the prison they decided we had to have I.D. badges. Brother
Tom is 6' 2" tall.
Lady: Weight?
Me: 208
Lady: *type, type, type.* Height?
Me: 5' 11 3/4"
Lady: I don't have room to put all that. Is it o.k. with you if I just put 5'
12"?
Me: Uh, yeah its o.k. with me.
Lady: *type, type, type.*
Me: I like being different.
Brother Tom: I'm 5' 14"
Lady: Oh no!
I still have the chaplain's badge that says I'm 5' 12".

Coincidence: The next time I renewed my driver's license, I didn't notice until the following day, but the height was listed as 2 feet. I guess I shouldn't have told that first lady I liked being different. But I love it. Heavenly Father, thanks for the memories.

When our youngest, Jon-Michael, was 8 years old, he read in the Book of Revelations that whoever reads that book will receive a blessing. It is a hard book for anyone to read. So it should be hard for an eight year old. Well, he read it 8 times at age 8, and 8 years later he made a perfect 800 on the verbal (word, as in nourished by God's Word) section of the SAT. He took it two more times and the total became three perfect 800's. Why would the Lord be in something like that? Ask God. Or, just read the Book of Revelations once for however many years old you are, and the blessings might flow so full and running over that you have to ask God to stop. I don't know.

Thanksgiving weekend was over and I was driving Jon-Michael back to Georgia Tech. He talked about physics using words I had heard before, but had no idea what they really meant, not in the depth that he so fluently spoke. I told him I had a chapter in my book about physics, and I suspected he rolled his eyes as I kept looking at the road. I described my definition of inertia, hoping that he would not shatter the premise of my theories by pointing out some error in my simplistic definition, causing me to have to throw out what I had written. His response though, was more like something I would have said, "Another definition for inertia is just laziness."

I was relieved. I thought about the way I had used inertia in the book though, and laziness would not describe the inertia of spirit. Spirit simply does not have the ability to initiate change, so it is not laziness on the part of spirit. I suspect though, since God has provided us with both spirit and soul, the laziness might be attributed to the soul, in that, it is the soul's job to harness the spirit and then use it, and its power, for good.

Yes, our spirit and our soul are becoming one, but they are not yet one...and the soul in fact is the source of the laziness in man. Spirit has no ability to initiate change in its direction; soul has ability to influence the initiation of change in the spirit's direction. If we fail to change, if we fail to repent, it is the soul that is falling down on the job, as the spirit, which may well be the culprit in bad behavior, the spirit is locked into its present path, and therefore is one hundred percent dependent on the soul. The two grow together on earth, and become one eventually, but not yet. That is why, for good, God must sometimes allow us to bear afflictions that bring a broken and contrite heart. So we had better work on the laziness that keeps us from "reining-in" the spirit. Then God won't have to.

I said all that to say this: It is imperative that the soul (being the birthplace and habitat of love) be pro-active to harness the spirit and all its power. If you are about to do something because you are about to do something, that is not a good enough reason. Any little thing that tickles the soul, can trigger the spirit to lead off in the wrong direction. Then the soul becomes just a follower. The soul needs to quit being lazy. The soul has the absolute ability to redirect and lead the spirit, with the help of the Holy Spirit. The soul needs to *rein* in the spirit, and *reign*, in the spirit to allow the Holy Spirit to *rain* blessings of joy.

Jon-Michael is noted for saying memorable, and remarkable things, like "More people are unusual than usual." And another time when Francie told him, "You need to pick up your speed," he replied, "Speed is an abstract concept which cannot be lifted."

> Then Jesus said to them, "When you lift up the Son of Man, then you will know that I am He, and that I do nothing of Myself; but as My Father taught Me, I speak these things. And He who sent Me is with Me. The Father has not left Me alone, for I always do those things that please Him" (John 8:28-29).

Humble yourselves in the sight of the Lord, and He will lift you up (John 4:10).

It would be so easy to be proud of my four children. I am pleased with them. I do not want any part of Lucifer's pride. When John had finished baptizing Jesus, God said, "This is my Son, in whom I am well pleased." All four of my children have accepted Jesus as their savior, and nothing could please me more.

No two snowflakes are alike, and it seems like everyone I know real well is factually, a classic, and I love them. I don't know how God can possibly love every classic in the world, since every person is one, but He does, and He does it with Amazing Grace.

The blessing on my life will get me to where I'm supposed to be. Our family has been So, So, blessed.

I don't know when He did it
I did not hear a sound
I feel God's presence everywhere
For it is all around.

To all Papa Julian's descendants and all Brother Tom's descendants - and descendants here means by blood, by adoption, and by marriage, because that's how the Bible defines family - never forget, we are so, so blessed. It is important to know that you are blessed. Otherwise you could not be like David and be polite enough to give God thanks for you and your family's being so blessed. David, a descendant of Abraham, went from shepherd boy, to giant slayer, to king, and eventually to His destiny as an instrument in writing the one book that factually is, the inerrant Word of God.

Somebody said Satan does not attack us because of where we are. He attacks because of where we are going. I wrote, "Sometimes a thing's purpose can only be guessed at by asking, 'What did it do'?" So a child who shows great promise for the Lord will likely be greatly attacked by Satan. But the blessing of God will prevail. It may take decades, or not, but the blessing of God will prevail. Omniscience, Omnipotence, Omnipresence, and Perfect Love, all rolled into One, will see to that.

Sometimes I realize I don't believe strongly enough some things that I believe. It is at those times I need to stop and thank the Lord for reminding me to draw closer to Him, and in that closeness I feel His love, and I linger, and my belief is renewed by the presence of His overwhelming love, and the love of his overwhelming presence.

I first come through the gate with thanksgiving, because even when I am carnally minded I can still truthfully thank the Lord for

162

something that just came to mind. Just thanking Him that I can always come to Him is enough to get me in the gate. After getting inside, let the praise begin. Draw me nearer, nearer, nearer, Blessed Lord - He inhabits my praise. His love inhabits me in the glow of His presence.

I went to the rest room about 10:30 a.m. and while there I realized I had not been acknowledging God's presence during the two hours I had been at work. I immediately thanked Him for reminding me. That thanksgiving got me inside the gate. I immediately felt His presence and praised Him for His system of using Proverbs 3: 6, the way He does. I thanked Him for doing it, not thanking Him to get inside the gate where I already was. I was thanking Him because I simply wanted to thank Him for that, that I acknowledged Him, in combination with thanksgiving and praise. I then acknowledged that even me immediately thanking Him for reminding me was likely His doing, sort of a nice circle. His presence was such a reminder of how easy it is to assure oneself of being spiritually minded rather than carnally minded. "I hope y'all are paying attention!"

Keep your eye on the big picture, with your ear toward the still small voice.

THE CENTER OF THE BIBLE:

There are 594 chapters before Psalm 117.
There are 594 chapters after Psalm 117.
So Psalm 117 is .the center of the Bible.
Guess what.
Psalm 117 is the shortest chapter in the Bible.

That seems remarkable. What are the odds of that happening by coincidence? God did it on purpose, that's the long and the short of it.

Remember the greatest commandment is to love God with all our heart and pretty much everything else we have? But no, Psalm 117 doesn't say that. It gives us the key tool to help us do that. God inhabits the praises of His people, and that benefits us. God loves us so, so much that He wants what's best for us. He wants to spend time with us and for us to spend time with Him. If we spend that quality time, our love grows. So in Psalm 117 (KJV) He says:

O praise the LORD, all ye nations: praise him, all ye people.

For his merciful kindness is great toward us: and the truth of the LORD endureth for ever. Praise ye the LORD.

A reason for this *coincidence* is suggested above. But sometimes what God does may be called "hiding Easter eggs." More about that after the following words from Jesus.

Then Peter came to Him and said, "Lord, how often shall my brother sin against me, and I forgive him? Up to seven times?"

Jesus said to him, "I do not say to you, up to seven times, but up to seventy times seven (Matthew 18:21-22).

When Jesus responded, "...up to 70 times 7." He wasn't asking Peter to do the math. Forget about the math. His answer was not really, "Forgive him up to 490 times". He was asking Peter to grasp the concept. I think the 70 multiple of 7 stood for God's perfect love that found a way to forgive eternally.

Never forget, bad actions have bad consequences, but that was not the question. The question was about forgiveness. True repentance, in Christ, brings true forgiveness from God every time. And we should seek to forgive like God. But God did better than we can do. God gave the gift that keeps on giving - Sinless Jesus on the cross - and the gift that keeps on forgiving - Glorious Jesus, the Risen Savior. The blood of the Risen Savior is greater than my sin. As with many things in the Bible, don't worry about the math. Grasp the concept. And remember to grasp the concept of Love in God's forgiveness whenever you eat eggs for breakfast.

How many days does it take for an egg to hatch?

Potato bug	7 (7)
canary	14 (7+7)
chicken	21 (7+7+7)

ducks and geese 28 (7+7+7+7)

except mallard   35 (7+7+7+7+7)

parrot and ostrich 42 (7+7+7+7+7+7)

Why all the 7's? Is it because evolution has feelings, and evolution likes to communicate, and evolution orchestrates *coincidences*, and evolution likes the number 7?

I don't think so! That seems less than a "*week*" case for evolution...as 7 days have been in every *week*, since the beginning of time, having been established by God and God alone. There is no physics reason causing a week to have 7 days. It has 7 days because God declared 7 days - He described what He did on each of 7 days.

I think the eggs listed above, with special numbers, show God likes to hide "Easter eggs" - eggs for his children to find, and when they find them, it gives them joy, because then they can hear Him saying, "I'm still here, and I love you." God is still sending His Word to us today, in His mercy, in His love, in His grace, speaking to us face to face, touching our hearts, healing our souls, and even our bodies through the knowledge of His presence.

The Book of Revelation describes Satan's 'number' as 666 and Jesus' 'number' as 777.

Do you remember chicken eggs take 21 days to hatch, and 21, like Jesus, is also 7+7+7?

That's no coincidence.
Jesus told me to say
He eats at Chick-fil-A !

Just trying to see if you are paying attention. And this leads into information about the founder of Chick-fil-A, a billionaire man of God named Truett Cathy, to discuss here and then more thoroughly in Chapter 13.

Truett Cathy and R.O.M.E.O.

On October 12, 1994, *I happened* to be doing an audit of Blue Ridge Conference on Leadership, in midtown Atlanta, Georgia, when the executive director, Bob Eskew, invited me to lunch. Over a period of decades this was the only time he did that. We went to his church, First Presbyterian Church of Atlanta, which was nearby. They were having their annual Business & Professional Luncheon, and Truett Cathy was the guest speaker. I met Mr. Cathy, the founder of Chick-fil-A, again some years later. Francie and I were having lunch at Matthews Cafeteria in midtown Tucker, Georgia, on Main Street at the railroad tracks. It must have been for Valentine's Day, or something, since I don't normally have lunch during the week. I don't know why Mr. Cathy of Chick-fil-A was there, either, but I suspect he was friends with the owners. You know what people say, "Chicks of a feather flock together."

As I write this, Bob Eskew lives in a retirement village in Austell, Georgia. Somewhere near the same timeframe that Francie and I went to Matthews, Bob Eskew e-mailed me that he had just visited Tucker, to eat at Matthews Cafeteria. No one else ever e-mailed me anything like that before. And I don't normally eat lunch during the week. So Truett Cathy's and Bob Eskew's trip to Matthews are on my "God's Hand versus *coincidences"* list, with God mostly saying, "Hi Bill, I'm still here, and I love you."

It seems Bob is a member of R.O.M.E.O. That stands for "Retired Older Men Eating Out," and the bus load of members came to Matthews in Tucker because of its reputation for great country food. No atmosphere, it's all about the food and the price is good, so Matthews is the highlight of any trip to midtown Tucker, Georgia.

So Hooray for R.O.M.E.O., and hooray for LOVE, and another episode to KNOW LOVE!

Isaiah 41:10:

Fear not, for I am with you;
Be not dismayed, for I am your God.
I will strengthen you,
Yes, I will help you,
I will uphold you with My righteous right hand.

Andy Rooney said, "I've learned that it's those small daily happenings that make life so spectacular."

Yesterday a football game was on TV, but it was not one I was interested in. I had just opened a battered and worn KJV Bible that I hadn't opened in maybe ten years. I have had two new ones since I last used it. There was a yellow "post-it" sticker that marked a page in Leviticus. I started looking to see what I had thought was worth coming back to ten or twenty years ago, in Leviticus of all places.

I was reading Chapter 25 verse 22, "And ye shall sow the eighth year, and eat yet of old fruit until the ninth year; until her fruits come in ye shall eat of the old store...." The TV caught my attention, as I thought the announcer said, "This year he has five Russian touchdowns, and he is about to come in now." At exactly the same time that I read "come in" the announcer said, "come in" - I noticed the coincidence and as I thought, I realized he said 'rushing touchdowns,' not Russian touchdowns, and I laughed at myself.

Then within about fifteen seconds, I was reading in verse 19, continuing to skim around trying to determine what was the reason I marked the page ten or twenty years ago, and I read, "And the land shall yield her fruit, and ye shall eat your fill, and dwell therein in safety."

And at the exact instance I read the word "safety," the announcer said the word "safety," referring to a particular player's position.

I still don't know why I marked that page to come back to ten or twenty years ago. Do you? My story of "the five Russian touchdowns" and "come in" - "safety" - would not be conclusive by themselves, but combined with the frequency of *coincidences* I see, I am compelled to offer you the opportunity to consider my perspective, just in case it might help you to better seek to delight in the Lord, and have the Lord delight in you.

> There are many who say,
> "Who will show us any good?"
> LORD, lift up the light of Your countenance upon us.
> You have put gladness in my heart...
> Psalm 4:6-7a.

You delight in your children when they acknowledge the *fact* of your presence? Then obey Proverbs 3:6 KJV, "In all thy ways acknowledge him and he shall direct thy paths." Allow your Father to delight in you! If you went to a lot of trouble to get your children's attention, would you rather they ignore you? As my teacher said, try to let any error be on the side of overestimating God rather than underestimating Him, because you can't overestimate Him.

How could omnipotent God orchestrate the coincidences? I quickly think of a couple of ways, and one seems more likely than the other. However, remembering throughout the Bible and particularly Proverbs 3:5 KJV, "Trust in the Lord with all thine heart; and lean not unto thine own understanding," the focus doesn't need to be on the *how* God does it. The focus needs to be on the *Who* that does it. And the focus needs to be on acknowledging God when He is the Who Who does it. Why? If you were invisible wouldn't you want your children to acknowledge you? Particularly if that would be to their great benefit. Wouldn't you do little things to get their attention, to help them get practice acknowledging you in the little things, so they would spend time with you, would delight in you, and could better let you guide them in the big things?

Our son Jon-Michael grew up hearing his sister's many poems, songs and stories. On Easter, 1991, when he was three years old, he told Francie he wanted to write a poem, and for her to take dictation, so she did. She wrote exactly what he said, and when she read it back to him, he heard a mistake he had made in the last line. She did not change it. It seems to us more precious this way.

EASTER: AGE THREE

God is Love.
And you are you.

And God loves you.
And God is true.

And God is good.
And God is straight.
He straights His Arms out. (on the cross)
And God is great.

And God loves you.
And He loves me, too.

And you and me loves God.

****

When Francie saw her poems, and the children's poems in KNOW LOVE early on, she said, "You're letting other people write your book for you!"

Well duh! As she knows, that's what accepting gifts from the Lord is all about. I can't write a book on my own. That's what family is for. The family of God knows, "We're all in this together."

Walking with the Lord is about using the gifts God has bestowed upon us, and sharing them with others. No, I don't steal poems from

172

women and children. I have their permission - even Jon-Michael's. After all, as I write this he needs the remainder of his senior year at Georgia Tech to be paid for. So he is probably receiving the highest price ever negotiated for a poem dictated by a three-year-old.

Three Ways To Give Physical Life

In your 10/2 issue, Sam Callaway made the same mistake as my three-year-old son.

My wife turned around and saw Jon-Michael grabbing candy from a store bucket.

She shrieked, "You can't do that!"

He responded, "But it says it's free!"

The sign said, "Sugar Free."

I'm proud my three-year-old can read the word "free." But a little bit of reading can be a dangerous thing.

Likewise, without meaning to be demeaning, I'm happy that Mr. Callaway used the Bible as his authority in trying to support his pro-abortion stand. The Bible says that study of God's word is the way to please God. But Mr. Callaway needs to read the rest of the story.

He is right, Genesis 2:7 does say, "And the Lord God formed man of the dust of the ground and breathed into his nostrils the breath of life, and man became a living soul." But that has nothing to do with the subject.

Genesis 2:7 just shows the point at which life went into Adam's blood. But Adam was not created by the combining of a sperm and an egg the way "us babies" were. According to the book *Chemistry of the Blood*, the father's sperm carries the blood chromosome which determines the baby's blood.

It's the blood that carries the oxygen from the lungs to the cells of the body which must have it to live. (Lev. 17:11 says, "For the life of the flesh is in the blood.")

After Adam, life was passed from generation to generation by the blood of Adam being passed on.

The Bible tells us that Jesus, like Adam, also did not have an earthly father. So for the second time in history a man's body was created without the necessity of sperm from an earthly father.

Mr. Callaway took one verse and incorrectly assumed life always begins that way...when breathing through the lungs begins. But oxygen is carried through the placenta to the baby's blood while she is still in the womb.

In summary, there have been at least three ways of giving physical life to men. I've mentioned the Adam way, the Baby Jesus way, and "the rest of us babies" way. (Of course, when God made Eve, He was just ribbing Adam.)

Finally, Mr. Callaway relegated "a fetus" to the status of "a tumor."

Luke 1 draws a beautiful picture that says by contrast, "a tumor never jumped for joy." John the Baptist did, in his mother's womb! He did it when the "mother," Baby Jesus, entered the house in His mother's womb. "The babe jumped for joy," is what it says.

Read Luke chapter 1. It's beautiful. And it's free...Sugar.

William J. (Bill) Ivey Tucker

Chapter 13:

The Greatest Commandment

You shall love the LORD your God with all your heart, with all your soul, and with all your strength. And these words which I command you today shall be in your heart. You shall teach them diligently to your children, and shall talk of them when you sit in your house, when you walk by the way, when you lie down, and when you rise up. You shall bind them as a sign on your hand, and they shall be as frontlets between your eyes. You shall write them on the doorposts of your house and on your gates (Deuteronomy 6:5-9).

"Teacher, which is the great commandment in the law?" Jesus said to him, " 'You shall love the LORD your God with all your heart, with all your soul, and with all your mind" (Matthew 22:36-37).

When God revealed the Greatest Commandment, He wasn't commanding our love just for Himself. He was commanding it for Himself *because* it would be for our good. He was *putting us first*, not because He needed our love, but *because* we needed to give it to Him, we needed to love Him to maximize our own benefits. Jesus wasn't proclaiming the commandment from on high, written in tablets of stone. Jesus was asked a question, and He answered the question truthfully. It wasn't Jesus seeking the love, it was Jesus giving an honest answer. That is the way love would prefer to do it. Why? Because love is not self-seeking and love rejoices in truth.

What does "greatest" in "Greatest Commandment" mean? *If we, of our own God given free will, will just follow that one, all the others will fall into place, as well as a lot of benefits to everyone on a grand scale.*

In his book, *It's Easier To Succeed Than To Fail*, Chick-fil-A founder, billionaire Truett Cathy wrote, "It's how you handle problems that makes the difference, not whether you have problems." Jesus already told us we will have problems. Right after Cathy's second store burned down, he had the added burden of needing surgery. That was when he learned the hard way he was allergic to codeine. The surgery took place but the polyps grew back, and he had to have greater surgery. He had problems. He and the Lord handled them the right way.

You already know Mr. Cathy succeeded in the business world. How did he do in the family world? Mr. Cathy bought his oldest son a car, and presented it on his eighteenth birthday, with a nameplate on the dash that said, "Custom made for DAN CATHY, Matthew 6:33." Matthew 6:33 says, "But seek ye first the kingdom of God, and his righteousness; and all these things will be added unto you" (KJV).

Seek to be aware of the Lord at all times. Don't let your performance be the motivating factor in your day. This is important. If you succeed with a good performance it can invite pride that you don't deserve. If your performance is poor, you can become discouraged. To borrow a wake up call from Dr. Charles Stanley, about here he might say, "Listen." You are His workmanship. Acknowledge His presence. It is rude to ignore people. Let His presence and your mutual love be the motivating force. Secondarily though certainly, seek for righteousness to fall into place. In mutual love, seek His performance in your life, and in you. That is the heart of the Kingdom of God.

When it came time for the next two children to have cars, they insisted on nameplates inside their cars too. Trudy chose Luke 1:37, "For with God nothing is impossible." (KJV). Way to go Trudy! Actually Bubba came before Trudy, and I chose to report his choice last because, yes, Bubba chose Deuteronomy 6:5, "And thou shalt love the Lord thy God with all thine heart, and with all thy soul, and with all thy might" (KJV). Mr. Cathy wrote, "A flood of joy swept through me because my almost eighteen-year-old son requested such words to be placed on his auto."

One swept through me too, as I read that, because the Lord had given me such an episode near the end of writing this book. Really. I had been waiting for weeks for Cathy's book to come. Francie ordered it after she read the "Truett Cathy and R.O.M.E.O." episode. I had left space in this chapter for potential comments from his book, but Bubba's request caught me by surprise. And I loved it. Oh how I loved it!

Think about it. God has infinite wisdom. As I write this, Mr. Cathy is now 88 years old. I think Mr. Cathy, a Sunday School teacher and perfect role model for life success lessons to young boys, saw early in life how God has things constructed. God has them constructed such that doing right pays better in the long run than does the other alternative. The ultimate "right" is to love God back. I mean, come on, understand God has infinite wisdom and we don't. If you could see the future like God can, you could buy and sell stock every minute and have gains every minute of the day so that you could easily become a billionaire very quickly. So how would omniscient, omnipotent God use the ability to see the future? In the spiritual universe, God would fix it such that - even though for every action there is an equal and opposite reaction in physics, and even though we CPA's will tell you if you don't have debits equal tocredits you will be out of balance - God has things fixed so that good wins in the long run.

How does He do that? Well, number one, He did it by making a great sacrifice. But He even did that with infinite wisdom, knowledge, power, love, and a bunch of other qualities that we can't hold a candle to. He paid a very high price of "good" to equal all our "bad." As a CPA, I speculate that's how things stay in balance in the spiritual universe. We owed a debt we could not pay, so He paid a debt He did not owe. He paid it with love, for us. And sweat. And blood.

Now if we want to keep on breaking the greatest commandment and not love Him with everything we've got, how smart are we? I mean, He has disclosed to us the "greatest" key to joy and to success. If we don't use that key, just how smart are we?

God is omniscient and yet, even though we don't deserve it, He loves us with all His heart, all His soul, all His strength, all His might, and all His mind, and His blood, so He hung on the cross. And He is risen!

Robyn wrote a related song many years ago which conveys priceless love in both the words and the tune. Unfortunately I cannot convey its extraordinarily lovely and at the same time exciting tune in the words of this book. But you can read its meaningful lyrics as follows:

HE ROSE AGAIN

He was beaten
Almost stoned
He's the true one of the throne

and He suffered
a great loss
when He was nailed to the cross

But He died for you and me
so we could live eternally

In human body, He felt the pain
Then He rose again

If that isn't love
then what could love truly be
more than words can explain
He even died for you and me

He even died for you and me...

But He rose again
Oh, yes, He rose again
Why are you searching here for Him?
He is not here
He's not among the dead.
"He's alive and well"
That's what the angel said.

HE IS RISEN!

Chapter 14:

Conclusion from *Know Love*

GIVEN: (1) The greatest thing a person can do is love God with all his heart, plus with everything else he has. (2) God doesn't call the equipped. He equips the called.

When I started this book, I thought the whole book was going to be about God creating us because of love. Brother Tom is a stickler for "rightly dividing the Word," and Isaiah's statement in the Old Testament that God created us for His glory didn't seem to me to jive with two other passages. The New Testament statements in 1 John 4:8 and 1 Corinthians 13 say "God is love" and "love is not self-seeking." Since I knew all three passages would be inerrant, I knew there had to be a reconciliation somewhere, and the Lord showed me where it was, as explained in Chapter 16.

Then, after that, I thought instead it was going to be mostly about the Greatest Commandment. I have often wondered, since there is a Greatest Commandment, why don't people talk about it more? We didn't do so well on that question. Or did we? I learned that remembering love, while in the journey of life, blesses my heart, and I know it blesses the heart of God.

Finally, I just ran across something a friend, David Montgomery, wrote. David was a brilliant local attorney, and like me, was a member of Northlake Kiwanis Club in Tucker. He gave up a prosperous law practice to become a missionary to Russia for quite a few years. Then he attended seminary in the USA, and the last I heard was serving the Lord at a church in another state. He wrote about "Three levels of obedience." They were fear of punishment, desire for blessings, and love for God. All three are a necessary fact of life for God to grow us, and for us to raise our children. His writings showed that the greatest of the three is love. We should attempt to raise our children, as they become old enough, to be obedient to us, yes, for all three reasons, but most of all because of love. And we, as His children, as we become mature enough, should seek to be obedient to Him because of love for Him. And I suspect He is helping us do that right now.

But I didn't reach the answer I was looking for. "Why doesn't the Greatest Commandment get more attention?" I can only speculate that since Love is not self-seeking, Satan is able to downplay that commandment, and to use a perspective set forth by a pastor at Rehoboth: Satan smothers the truth, so that the greatest commandment has no oxygen. That limits the power of God in God's people, and they are spiritually destroyed over a period of generations, for a lack of knowledge. Actually, Hosea 4:6 proclaims an extremely strong message on the subject:

> My people are destroyed for lack of knowledge.
> Because you have rejected knowledge,
> I also will reject you from being priest for Me;
> Because you have forgotten the law of your God,
> I also will forget your children.

I want to encourage you to go back to the beginning of Chapter 13 and read again Deuteronomy 6:5-9, and take to heart the helpful verses 6-9. God gave us those words from His infinite wisdom, because of His infinite love for us. Those verses don't just state the commandment; they command us with helpful details on how to grow the love in our children, and in future generations.

Can you just imagine how a nation's culture and its numbers of Godly people would decline from my grandpa's generation to your grandchildren's generation in the absence of people following Deuteronomy 6:5-9? Well, it is happening. The business world and the media know that the more publicity a product receives, the more people buy it. God knew that before they did. He knew it when He wrote Deuteronomy 6:5-9. If nobody talks about a product (and Deuteronomy

6:5-9 is a product - the most important product in the history of the world), it dies a slow death. Or at least it has to be hooked up to an oxygen tank. I agree with focusing on the Gospel. The most beautiful time of my trips to prison was when I held hands with seven inmates in a circle and led them to the Lord, and next trip there, one of them ran up to me joyfully telling that he had led someone to the Lord. I became a granddaddy in a spiritual sense, when that person he told me about was "born again." But with disobedience to, and without focus on Deuteronomy 6: 5-9, there may not be many of our own children/grandchildren in a next generation of "focus-ers" to spread the Gospel.

At its utmost, the Great Commission ("Go tell") is a response to the Greatest Commandment (Love God). The Great Commission must put forth the Greatest Commandment more explicitly, more publicly and more gloriously, if it, the Great Commission, is to fulfill its highest purpose.

The Great Commission is great. But the Greatest Commandment is called the greatest for a reason, and if we don't talk about *that* product the product becomes virtually obsolete while

the
competitor's
inferior
and
toxic
products
steal
market share.

Throughout our history this nation has benefited from the promise, "Blessed is the nation whose God is the Lord" (Psalm 33:12). What will be the way to restore our land to its position of blessedness? II Chronicles 7:14 gives a well-publicized formula. "If My people who are called by My name will humble themselves, and pray and seek My face, and turn from their wicked ways, then I will hear from heaven, and will forgive their sin and heal their land." But there is another emphasis to consider: emphasis on the Greatest Commandment. Emphasis on Christians' loving God with everything we have will activate II Chronicles 7:14.

A revival is what II Chronicles requires, and destitute people can be brought to revival more easily than comfortable people. But if leading Christians, from pulpits across the nation, will focus on the Greatest Commandment, more and more Christians (God's people) will get the message. That will be a more effective way to bring revival than stepping in, in destitute times, with the II Chronicles message to repent.

Why do I say that? America is a huge ship to turn around. Turning from wicked ways requires motivation, as does loving God, "So So much". David praised God and spoke of loving God much more than of repentance. He spoke of repentance. He agreed with God when God chastised him. But it was not the central theme. And I submit that loving God is a more thoroughly inviting message for Christians in America, than repentance, and the end result is - repentance.

II Chronicles 7:14 describes what we have to do. Deuteronomy 6:5-9 describes how to do it. You can say that again! II Chronicles 7:14 describes what we have to do. Deuteronomy 6:5-9 describes how to do it!

So having said all of that, still, I leave you with this conclusion, to borrow a perspective from Frank Daniels, yesterday in Bible Fellowship Class at Rehoboth:

> In God's infinite wisdom, He created sheep with a tremendous ability to resist being 'herded' and instead to follow their shepherd. And Jesus said, "My sheep know my voice." Disciples are much more intelligent than sheep, and that makes it natural for disciples to follow their own intellect, whereas the Lord's sheep follow the Shepherd, and get the benefit of His infinite wisdom as He leads them down the right paths at the right time.

So I would seem to have gone full circle, and am back where I began when I was led to the Lord in February 1981. "Trust in the Lord

with all thy heart, lean not unto thine own understanding. In all thy
ways acknowledge Him, and He will direct thy paths."

P.S. In December 1981 the 'path' led to the other end of the buffet
table. The vision of her, like the first line of her fifth grade poem, said, "I
have the answer that you need." And the answer was love.

REPEAT OF:

**You shall love the LORD your God with all your heart, with
all your soul, and with all your strength.**

**And these words which I command you today shall be in your
heart. You shall teach them diligently to your children, and
shall talk of them when you sit in your house, when you walk
by the way, when you lie down, and when you rise up. You
shall bind them as a sign on your hand, and they shall be as
frontlets between your eyes. You shall write them on the
doorposts of your house and on your gates. (Deuteronomy 6:5-
9)**

They Sing 'Happy Birthday' Before Opening Gifts

It was Christmas 1981 and I lived in a lonesome bachelor apartment. My younger brother and his wife invited me to spend the night with them for Christmas Eve. I gladly did.

The next morning I witnessed a wonderful sight. We all gathered at the Christmas tree before daylight — they had small children.

Before any child went to a present, they did something I will always cherish being a part of. When you give someone a birthday party, you sing "Happy Birthday" before the presents are opened.

They sang "Happy Birthday" to Jesus, before daylight on Christmas morning.

My brother died in 1988. Now I am married to his wife's sister. In addition to my two grown sons, we have children ages eight and three. When we sing that song first thing this Christmas morning, likely tears of joy will run down my cheeks once more.

This may sound silly, but here are the words to the song. It might help someone experience the spirit of Christmas. It might help them remember to sing "Happy Birthday" at the birthday party at their house this Christmas.

Happy Birthday to You,
Happy Birthday to You,
Happy Birthday, Dear Jesus —
Happy Birthday to You.

Bill Ivey
Tucker

Chapter 15:

Grace

"Although God is love, love is not God, right?" I am going to

defer to Charles Spurgeon on that. If God only started with love, at that

point He would not be the other attributes. But God never started. He just

always has been, and always has had His other attributes, so I want to say

love is not God, even though God is love, and even though God is the

source of all love. However, on another level, the grace Spurgeon refers

to says to me that while God never changes (and He always has been and

always will be the same), it says to me that once Jesus had paid the price,

through grace, grace became God in that now grace is reigning. God

didn't change, but events took place and grace "activated" and became

God that God had always been. Perfect Grace had not previously taken

place, and was not previously reigning. Spurgeon spoke with such power

and grace and truth, reminiscent of John 1:14, that I am ready to say,

"Whatever Spurgeon says must be right."

Charles Spurgeon said, "...for it is written 'God is love,' which is

an *alias* for grace. Oh, come and bow before it; come and adore the

infinite mercy and grace of God. Doubt not, halt not, hesitate not. Grace is reigning; grace is God; God is love. Oh that you, seeing grace is thus enthroned, would come and receive it. I say, then, that grace is enthroned by conquest, by right, and by power...." Grace has paid the ultimate price, not to the exclusion of God's other attributes, but in the presence of God's other attributes grace reigns, and reigns supreme, by conquest, by right, and by power.

Spurgeon pointed to Jesus as being the definition of and embodiment of grace and Jesus being God, and therefore grace reigns as God because Jesus reigns. He said it more powerfully, more fully, and more accurately, with the gift God gave him for saying it. Spurgeon usually spoke extemporaneously. And in speaking he was clearly blessed with the presence of the Holy Spirit. You really must read, "The throne of grace. Hebrews 4:16," a sermon he delivered in 1871. It is the most powerful sermon I have ever experienced. So while I think my first paragraph above is correct, and not in contradiction to Spurgeon, in the presence of Spurgeon's words I am ready to quickly take a back seat at any hint of my being incorrect. Nothing should be allowed to detract from the truth of Spurgeon's words, grace is reigning. But please, do read the rest of Spurgeon's story, which is available on the internet. What his message means for each of us can be adequately explained only in the words he spoke so gloriously.

Meanwhile, think about it. Think about the triumphant joy in which grace is God. Think about the love that grace deserves from you. Think about the obedience God is entitled to from you, being entitled to 100% love for Him. Yes, think about the ramifications that grace is God! Any time we spend focusing on grace is time spent focusing on Jesus. And that is a good thing.

He is righteousness, and being also perfect love He would have to be righteousness, because unrighteousness has evil consequences, and perfect love could have no part in evil consequences. But perfect love did not cause God's righteousness, neither one caused the other, but each requires the other for each to exist, at His infinite level of perfection.

God is able to maintain all His infinitely positive attributes because the attributes He has are infinitely positive, and they complement each other, thereby we have an infinitely good, infinitely synergistic God, thereby infinitely fortified in every good way. "A Mighty Fortress is our God."

What God has done, in making us in His image, is give us the stuff to become like Him. Not equal to, but like. What God is doing in growing us here on earth, is growing us to be more like Him. More like perfection. He is growing us to have more love, more righteousness, etc., than when we began. We have the opportunity to bask in His glory, abiding with Him, as it helps us become more like Him. And obeying the Great Commission, giving truth to others, more abundantly grows that truth in us, as we become more like Him. But He has paid a horrible price for us to be able to do that.

Still, with love being the God-declared principle (John 3:16) in the price He paid, it is the principal principle we need to attempt to address. It is not the only principle of God, and it is not the only principle we need to address, but for us it is a prerequisite for developing toward the other omni-traits of the King of kings and Lord of lords.

"Love is an alias for grace." And you become like what you focus on most. Hence, the sheep need to focus, with ears to hear, on the Lamb of God. The sacrificed lamb is now the Shepherd. In His grace become more like the Shepherd, by being His sheep.

> I have loved you with an everlasting love; Therefore with loving-kindness I have drawn you (Jeremiah 31:3).

And he said unto them, Set your hearts unto all the words which I testify among you this day, which ye shall command your children to observe to do, For it is not a vain thing for you; because it is your life; and through this thing ye shall prolong your days in the land.... (Deut. 32: 46-47 KJV).

And Moses was an hundred and twenty years old when he died; his eye was not dim, nor his natural force abated (Deut. 34:7).

And that truly was a miracle, given Moses' life. But I see several amazing *coincidences* regarding Moses' living to be one hundred and twenty, with all the *coincidences* being clearly orchestrated by God.

1. Even though Pharoah ordered every male baby to be killed, Pharoah's own daughter saved the life of Moses, for him to become the baby of Pharoah's own daughter. Can you almost see that smile on God's face?

2. Pharoah's daughter paid Moses' own Mother to nurse baby Moses. God may still be laughing about that one!

3. God made Moses the leader of the Israelites, leading them away from Pharoah, the killer of babies Moses' age.

4. God spoke to His people through Moses, so during that time Moses clearly walked with God. Moses' living one hundred and twenty years on earth was no coincidence, and likely was a result of Moses "walking with God".

Remember, it is the high frequency of *coincidences* that makes it unlikely that they are *coincidences*. But number 2 above takes the cake as far as I am concerned.

When something like that, a "coincidence," happens today, be ready to acknowledge God's hand in it. Otherwise, you will not even come close to complying with Proverbs 3:6, "In all thy ways acknowledge Him, and He will direct thy paths." If you chalk it all up to coincidence, you will miss all the miracles and the joy of walking with the Lord directing your path.

Did you ever hear the expression, "God is in the details"? The first time I came close to hearing it was a Congressman saying about a proposed bill, "The Devil is in the details." Whenever coincidences attract your attention, look for God in that volume of coincidences, that bunch of details. And think about why He is showing them to you. He may be just saying, "Hi, yes, I am in that bunch of details, and I just wanted to say again, 'I love you." Or, He may be saying something else, something He will be happy to make clear to you if you ask Him. But, "I love you," coming directly from God is pretty good, right?

As the slogan went on the prison ministry trips, "If God's in it, you ain't got nothin' to worry about!"

Some things will not be revealed until we get to Heaven. Others are revealed by a close reading of the Bible. To paraphrase a very learned Biblical scholar, it is not until the very last verse of the Bible, Revelation

22:21 KJV, that God reveals He is a Southerner - as the Bible closes lovingly with the words

> The grace of the Lord Jesus Christ be with "you all." Amen.
> Quotation marks added, in a spirit of joy and appreciative love.

Interlude: Shh - Prayer in Progress – In Love

Thank you Lord for warming my heart. Sometimes just thinking about your presence makes my blood tingle.

> For the life of the flesh *is* in the blood, and I have given it to you upon the altar to make atonement for your souls; for it *is* the blood *that* makes atonement for the soul. (Leviticus 17:11)

Lord I know You love me, because You bought and paid for my soul with such a high price. Where can I find an owner's manual for operating my life? Could you write one for me? I get off track, and don't know how to turn things around.

> All Scripture *is* given by inspiration of God, and *is* profitable for doctrine, for reproof, for correction, for instruction in righteousness, that the man of God may be complete, thoroughly equipped for every good work. (2 Tim 3)

Lord, I know You are referring to the Bible. Thank you for that. It is a wonderful owner's manual as well as a love letter to your children. It said that you would send the Comforter, the Holy Spirit, and I know you did. But sometimes I don't feel comforted. What should I do? Could we talk about it? Could we talk about love?

> Then He said, "Take now your son, your only *son* Isaac, whom you love, and go to the land of Moriah, and offer him there as a burnt offering on one of the mountains of which I shall tell you." (Gen 22.2)

Father, I already told them You were testing Abraham, and Abraham passed the test. And that You then provided a lamb for Abraham's burnt offering. As stated in chapter seven, likely, Abraham did not know that in that incident, he was a physical picture of Spiritual God doing the same thing for us. And Abraham's son was a forerunner of Jesus, whose Father sacrificed His Son, "whom He loved," on the cross, for us. So You will never ask anyone to do that again, because, as Jesus said on the cross, "It is finished!"

> You shall love the LORD your God with all your heart, with all your soul, and with all your strength. (Dt. 6:5)

> And now, Israel, what does the LORD your God require of you, but to fear the LORD your God, to walk in all His ways and to love Him, to serve the LORD your God with all your heart and with all your soul, *and* to keep the commandments of the LORD and His statutes which I command you today for your good? Indeed heaven and the highest heavens belong to the LORD your God, *also* the earth with all that *is* in it. The LORD delighted only in your fathers, to love them; and He chose their descendants after them, you above all peoples, as *it is* this day. (Dt 10:12-15)

> 'And it shall be that if you earnestly obey My commandments which I command you today, to love the LORD your God and serve Him with all your heart and with all your soul...(Dt 11:13)

> Lord, Deuteronomy Chapter 11 has thirty-two verses, and I am

going to encourage readers to read them all, on their own, including the admonition of what happens if we do not earnestly abide by Chapter 11. That will allow us to cover more ground together right now.

> ...and if you keep all these commandments and do them, which I command you today, to love the LORD your God and to walk always in His ways, then you shall add three more cities for yourself besides these three, (Dt 19-9)

Lord, I know You are communicating a principle there, for us today, rather than cities, and I get the message, and there is plenty else that I need!

> And the LORD your God will circumcise your heart and the heart of your descendants, to love the LORD your God with all your heart and with all your soul, that you may live. The LORD your God will make you abound in all the work of your hand, in the fruit of your body, in the increase of your livestock, and in the produce of your land for good. For the LORD will again rejoice over you for good as He rejoiced over your fathers, if you obey the voice of the LORD your God, to keep His commandments and His statutes which are written in this Book of the Law, *and* if you turn to the LORD your God with all your heart and with all your soul. (Dt 30:6, 9-19)

Father, we have great motivation to love You. We should take Your words to...heart.

> I will love You, O LORD, my strength. (Ps 18:1)

> LORD, I have loved the habitation of Your house,
> And the place where Your glory dwells. (Ps 26:8)

> The LORD *is* near to those who have a broken heart,
> And saves such as have a contrite spirit. (Ps 34:18)

Lord, I know Demons are not contrite spirits. Just the opposite,

and worse. They literally are spiritual monsters. But they are powerless at

the command of Jesus, and His glorious spiritual presence. Mark Chapter

One describes a scene where Jesus was teaching in the synagogue.

> Then they went into Capernaum, and immediately on the Sabbath
> He entered the synagogue and taught. And they were astonished at
> His teaching, for He taught them as one having authority, and not
> as the scribes.
> Now there was a man in their synagogue with an unclean spirit.
> And he cried out saying, "Let *us* alone! What have we to do with
> You, Jesus of Nazareth? Did You come to destroy us? I know who
> You are—the Holy One of God!"
> But Jesus rebuked him, saying, "Be quiet, and come out of him!"
> And when the unclean spirit had convulsed him and cried out with
> a loud voice, he came out of him. Then they were all amazed, so
> that they questioned among themselves, saying, "What is this?
> What new doctrine *is* this? For with authority He commands even
> the unclean spirits, and they obey Him." And immediately His
> fame spread throughout all the region around Galilee. (Mark
> 34:21-28)

There is a spiritual principle there. The evil spirit inside the man

could recognize Jesus, and knew He was the Son of God. "People" there

did not know who He was. This is the same principle we saw when John

The Baptist and Jesus were both in their mothers' wombs in Luke Chapter

One, and John the Baptist leaped for Joy. He spiritually discerned the

presence of Jesus as Mary walked in the door.

It's like a spirit has the x-ray vision attributed to Superman, but the spirit is seeing and recognizing another spirit, which cannot be seen with human eyes. I thought of this as I was watching "Knight Rider" on Retro Television last night. The featured young lady was blind. As we know to expect, after she lost her vision years before, her other senses grew more sensitive. And so her hearing became extra keen. And the sensitivity of her hearing gave her the ability to discern perfectly, from a camera with audio, the owner of the voice that no one else could even hear, until they maximized the volume, much less identify. And the crime was solved.

That works in the other direction too. An unborn baby, and a born baby, have abilities that we do not have, like spiritual discernment. But they lose them as new senses, such as physical sight, begin to be used. A spiritual sense, and its sensitivity, is like a muscle in that you use it or you lose it. So when the baby begins to use newly needed physical senses, the spiritual senses do not seem as much needed, and they decline.

This principle may also be a first cousin to the principle in Jesus' declaration that in order to be saved, "you must be born again!" We just start all over, not to be similar to the spiritual being we were in the womb, we become completely new and different, spiritually. Now Jesus is on the throne, with our spirit born again, this time born of incorruptible seed, and our soul is more mature. The problem comes when the soul asserts its authority improperly.

If we have not yet been born again, when we reach the age of accountability spiritual "law" comes into force. Satan offers us something we want, after he uses some snake in the grass to entice us to want it, as with Eve. Little do we know that the price we pay to commit that one sin, is our soul. Our eternal, immortal soul. But here comes Roy Rogers, and Gene Autry, and the Lone Ranger, and the cavalry and the One who bought and paid for our soul with His blood at Calvary. God says, "Do you take this Savior to be your lawful wedded Savior?" and we say, "Yes, Lord! I do." Jesus and Calvary have saved the day, and have likely used Roy Rogers, Gene Autry, the Lone Ranger, and the cavalry in our youth to sow seeds of joy, because the seeds of joy have blossomed.

God, I know you do not break our hearts. But You allow us to go our own free will way, because we need a broken heart to see our spirit become contrite. Some of us actually need a broken heart? For the unsaved, our self-centered spirit, and our selfish heart, cannot accept that we need a savior. It cannot accept the truth. So we put things ahead of God. Even after we are born again, later we are likely to put things ahead of God. That's called "backsliding." You have untold blessings for us, and untold purposes for us, but we cannot receive them because their foundation is a spiritual foundation, and our *self sufficient* spirit, and stiff necked soul, are not willing to receive the Holy Spirit initially. That would require change of direction, i.e., overcoming inertia, AKA "repenting," or our spirit is unwilling to follow His guidance later, not willing to keep following the Shepherd as just His sheep. So our heart may require surgery, to reawaken spiritual discernment that we have allowed to be buried under the cares of the world, or that have been suppressed by the usual human body senses that we use every day in our physical world. God is omniscient, and if there were a better way for Him to grow us, rather than surgery on our heart, He would use the better way. But we can be sure, since our Father is the Master Surgeon, the absolutely best decisions for us will be made by Him for His children.

Also, the descendants of His servants shall inherit it,
And those who love His name shall dwell in it. (Ps. 69:36)

You who love the LORD, hate evil!
He preserves the souls of His saints;
He delivers them out of the hand of the wicked. (Ps. 97:10)

As he loved cursing, so let it come to him;
As he did not delight in blessing, so let it be far from him. (Ps. 109:17)

Lord, while that verse is not about the kind of love You bless, it deserves inclusion here, because surely no one reading this book would prefer a curse to a blessing. You seem absolutely clear on this message, whether it means foul language versus delight in Your blessings, or speaking actual curses on people versus delight in Your blessings. Readers are warned, "Don't curse". They should tell You of their delight in Your blessings, and You and they can delight in many more blessings from You.

Cursing seems to me the opposite of those grand verses that so remind me to try to remember to use gracious words whenever I can. When I combine John 1:1 with John 1:14, they say to me that when we say any word, we are sort of standing on Holy ground. That goes double once we have accepted Jesus and the Holy Spirit abides in us.

In the beginning was the Word, and the Word was with God, and the Word was God. (John 1:1)

And the Word became flesh and dwelt among us, and we beheld His glory, the glory as of the only begotten of the Father, full of grace and truth. (John 1:14)

There is an expression, "You become like what you focus on most." So I would say to my dear grandchildren, focus on Jesus, and indeed, and in deed, you will be full of grace and truth.

> Pray for the peace of Jerusalem:
> "May they prosper who love you.
> Peace be within your walls,
> Prosperity within your palaces." (Ps. 122:6-7)

> I love those who love me,
> And those who seek me diligently will find me. (Pr. 8:17)

> Hatred stirs up strife,
> But love covers all sins. (Pr. 10:12)

> Better *is* a dinner of herbs where love is,
> Than a fatted calf with hatred. (Pr. 15:17)

> A friend loves at all times,
> and a brother is born for adversity. (Pr. 17:17)

> He brought me to the banqueting house,
> And his banner over me *was* love. (S of S 2:4)

> Therefore the Lord Himself will give you a sign: Behold, the virgin shall conceive and bear a Son, and shall call His name Immanuel. (Isa 7:14)

> And she will bring forth a Son, and you shall call His name Jesus, for He will save His people from their sins.
> So all this was done that it might be fulfilled which was spoken by the Lord through the prophet, saying: "Behold, the virgin shall be with child, and bear a Son, and they shall call His name Immanuel," which is translated, "God with us." (Mat 1:21-23)

> For unto us a Child is born,
> Unto us a Son is given;
> And the government will be upon His shoulder.

And His name will be called
Wonderful, Counselor, Mighty God,
Everlasting Father, Prince of Peace. (Isa 9:6)

Father, I consider it fascinating that the prophet Isaiah gave us

those words seven hundred years before Christ was born.

He will feed His flock like a shepherd;
He will gather the lambs with His arm,
And carry *them* in His bosom,
And gently lead those who are with young. (Isa 40:11)

I am the good shepherd. The good shepherd gives His life for the
sheep. (Jn 10:11)

I gave My back to those who struck *Me,*
And My cheeks to those who plucked out the beard;
I did not hide My face from shame and spitting. (Isa 50:6)

Then they spat on Him, and took the reed and struck Him on the
head. And when they had mocked Him, they took the robe off
Him, put His *own* clothes on Him, and led Him away to be
crucified. (Mat 27:30-31)

Father, I see a pattern of Yours. In Genesis, we saw You draw a

physical picture, telling Abraham to sacrifice his son; but You were just

telling what You were going to do, though no one could exactly

understand that message, except in retrospect. Through Isaiah, we see

You telling what is going to happen. Then seven hundred years later it

happens. You tell things, and we can't grasp what You are saying, until

You have us ready to hear You. You must have given Isaiah pretty good

ears, and/or a supernatural pen.

But He *was* wounded for our transgressions,
He was bruised for our iniquities;
The chastisement for our peace *was* upon Him,
And by His stripes we are healed. (Isa 53:5)

He was oppressed and He was afflicted,
Yet He opened not His mouth;
He was led as a lamb to the slaughter,
And as a sheep before its shearers is silent,
So He opened not His mouth. (Isa 53:7)

Then Pilate said to Him, "Do You not hear how many things they testify against You?" But He answered him not one word, so that the governor marveled greatly. (Mat 27:13-14)

There is another example of your pattern, Father. It is like the old preacher said when he was asked about his style of preaching. "I tells 'um what I'm gonna tell 'um, then I tells 'um, then I tells 'um what I told 'um."

Likewise, You told us You were going to sacrifice Jesus on the cross for our sins, then You sacrificed Jesus on the cross for our sins, then You told us in John 3:16 and so many other places that You sacrificed Jesus on the cross for our sins. You even told us why. You love us and You tell us so. So what should we do?

If readers answered, "We should love God a lotta bit, and we should tell Him so," they're getting warm.

The LORD has appeared of old to me, *saying:* "Yes, I have loved you with an everlasting love; Therefore with lovingkindness I have drawn you...." (Jer 31:3)

I drew them with gentle cords,
With bands of love,
And I was to them as those who take the yoke from their neck.
I stooped *and* fed them. (Hos 11:4)

"I will heal their backsliding,
I will love them freely,
For My anger has turned away from him." (Hos 14:4)

Hate evil, love good;
Establish justice in the gate.
It may be that the LORD God of hosts
Will be gracious to the remnant of Joseph. (Am 5:15)

He has shown you, O man, what *is* good;
And what does the LORD require of you
But to do justly,
To love mercy,
And to walk humbly with your God? (Mic 6:8)

"Shh - Prayer in Progress – In Love" will continue after a short intermission. The primary focus will be the New Testament.

Interlude: Intermission

There will have to be an intermission, because while I was

finishing up, "Shh – Prayer in Progress – In Love," I messed up, and I

wanted to cry. In one click of the mouse, I had, by mistake, eliminated ten

pages of the book - ten pages.

Oh my darling, oh my darling
Oh my darling, Clemency
Thou art lost and gone forever,
Dreadful sorry, Clemency.

I got the clemency. Loving mercy seems a very easy requirement

to meet! (See Micah 6:8 at the end of the previous page.) The ten pages

were gone from the computer, but I had hard copy with pencil changes, so

it was not lost and gone forever. But I still wanted to cry. I told Francie by

e-mail what had happened, how stupid I had been in messing up. Her

timing was perfect as she said, "Remember what Scott Hudgens said, 'The

only people what don't make mistakes are those what don't never do

nothin.'"

I thanked her profusely. I had been working on the book so hard.

It was almost 6 p.m. on Saturday, and I was trying to get the book

finished before Christmas. I felt the time of Christmas Spirit would be the

ideal time to present the book to a publisher. Surely Robyn's Christmas

Poem would be most appreciated then. As with most of my life, I was working so hard trying to meet my goals.

Now, with the detour, needing to type the ten pages all over (Robyn started pitching in on that), needing to put in a whole lot of corrections and additions, and wanting so much to push forward with the pre-Christmas goal, and tears welling up in my face, I started laughing. I was reminded of one of Francie's favorite jokes. "If you want to make God laugh, just tell Him your plans."

Make God laugh? No way, right? Wrong. As the song goes about, "Smile and the whole world smiles with you," I am more than slightly believing that the Lord would have me tell you, "In good humor, laugh and the Lord your God laughs with you!" More about that in the New Testament section of, "Shh – Prayer in Progress – In Love."

Meanwhile, you might want to know something about asking God today, to do things yesterday. He can.

Let's say you are all grown up. You have children. One of them is not home and it is getting very, very late. Can you pray that nothing bad has happened? Yes. But you don't think God is going to change something that has already happened for you do you? You can't pray that something in the past didn't happen, can you? You are not asking God to change history. You are asking Him to hear you in the past, to change

that future. If you pray, "Please heal my wife's cancer," that is a prayer

today, about the future, not the past.

But, picture this. God knew yesterday you would pray tonight. He

even knew what you would pray. So, now it is so late, and you have not

heard whether anything bad has happened, and you are concerned. So you

do pray to your Father, Almighty God, tonight, asking God to hear you

yesterday. You ask Him to provide yesterday for your child's safety

tonight, even though your child might otherwise have been in an accident

by now, but you do pray now. God could hear it yesterday. God can do

that stuff. Really. So He could set things in motion yesterday, to helpfully

affect things tonight. So do what you can for your child. We serve an

awesome God.

But would He do such a thing? I don't know, but two things tell

me to pray it; one, your child's life is potentially at stake, so how much

would it cost you to seek to buy safety insurance from God that way? And

two, I expect He would very much like to honor such a prayer that

acknowledges He has such great power to do such a thing, like nobody

else can.

If I pray that, thereby honoring God with my request (!), and my child comes home safely, likely I will never know if God honored the prayer. But I will know I did what I could for my child.

That principle is not restricted to your children. The principle of praying today, for God to hear you in the past, would apply to most anything. For example, you could pray, "Oh Father, thank you that I can come to you at a time like this, at Joe's funeral. It was such a shock hearing about the automobile accident. I praise you that you can hear me in the past, and act in the past on today's request. Lord, I tried to reach Joe, but I never found a way to get him to listen to me about Jesus. As best I could tell, Joe was lost and going to hell. But only you know for sure. Father, I pray that sometime, somewhere, some way, someone did reach Joe, and Joe came to a saving knowledge of the Lord Jesus Christ. Joe seemed lost. But I pray that what seemed like a lost man was just Joe's lack of Biblical knowledge, combined with his unique personality, and that I will see Him again when I get to heaven. I love you in the past and the present. In Jesus' name I pray. Amen."

But certainly don't count on doing that later, instead of while Joe is still alive. Now is the time to pray for Joe. Later would just be the desperation pass the football world calls a "Hail Mary," throwing the ball fifty yards down field into the end-zone with the ball up for grabs equally by either team, with no time left on the clock. Now is the time. Don't risk time running out for Joe.

<3 <3 <3 <3

Someone said, "Holding a grudge is like swallowing poison, hoping it will kill the person you are mad at."

Hanging on the cross, with spikes in His hands, a gash in His side, a torn and battered body, thorns sunk deeply into His head, the King of kings and Lord of lords, made a final request. "Forgive." So how can we call Him, "Lord," if we do not forgive?

If someone is holding a grudge, are they being spiritually minded or carnally minded? You know. One is life and the other is death. Because He loves you, the Lord wants you to choose life. And you do too.

Now I would say particularly to my dear grandchildren, and brother Bob's, and my sister Jean's, and whosoever will listen, do you have a problem that just won't go away? Let the problem be your tutor, because it is. Learn from that. Thinking of it that way also takes power away from it.

And though the Lord gives you
The bread of adversity and the water of affliction,
Yet your teachers will not be moved into a corner anymore,

But your eyes shall see your teachers.
Your ears shall hear a word behind you, saying,
" This is the way, walk in it,"
Whenever you turn to the right hand
Or whenever you turn to the left. (Isaiah 30:20-21)

Maybe my wiping out all those pages was so I would think to tell you how to perceive problems. Perceive them as tutors. But now you see you should do as I say, not as I do, because I am still learning, still being tutored. I think that, because I have told you about Isaiah 30:20-21, I will remember it better the next time I have a problem.

During my decades at Rehoboth Baptist Church in Tucker, I have learned from the teaching of five senior pastors, Lester Buice, Richard Lee, Bobby Atkins, Rusty Womack, and now Troy Bush. And I learned from the television teaching of Charles Stanley, and the companionship teaching of Brother Tom Norton.

Robyn is twenty-six now. Because of the learning from my trips to prison, two days after Bob passed away with ALS, I had the privilege of leading her to the Lord, when she was a very bright and mature four years old. It was at night-night time. Each night at bed-time the four of us would sing a song together, then we would each say a memory verse from the Bible, then I would make up, on the spot, a story. It would be about "Leap Rabbit," or some other creative character that children might like, but it would always have sweetness, or something else that should be sown in precious hearts, and it would have "funness," and excitement, as best I could do, with the Lord's great leading. Leap Rabbit somehow used his long ears like helicopter blades, to be able to fly. Up in the air! Then we would pray.

My most frequently used memory verse was Proverbs 3:5-6. I had used it many times. But on this night, when I finished my turn, for the first time, Robyn said, "What does that mean?" I explained each phrase of it, better than I ever could have before that time, or after, and Robyn said, "I want to invite Jesus into my heart." I looked at her mother, and her mother looked at me, and nodded yes, and I did it. I told her to repeat after me, and she accepted Jesus as her savior. You will see similar words in plenty of places in this book, just keep your eyes open for them.

Robyn wasn't green fruit. She was ready, and that was good. There was a time when her mother and I knew she really was too young. Dr. Charles Stanley had paved the way for us when she was less than two years old. I walked through the den, she was sitting on the sofa, Dr. Stanley on television was saying, "Now repeat after me..." and she did. Though Francie and I agreed she was too young then, and though it is unlikely, it still is possible that Robyn was Dr. Stanley's youngest convert ever. Praise the Lord!

My favorite humor may have been when Robyn was even younger. Oh, by the way, she knew the alphabet at thirteen months old. She had magnetic letters of the alphabet that she used to stick to the refrigerator. Once she came up to her mother and reached out, saying, "Ya wa a cup a tea?" It was the letter "T" in a cup, and she knew exactly what she was doing. I think learning and love thrive best in a spirit of good humor.

214

Interlude:

Shh – Prayer in Progress – In Love: continued - forever

New Testament Overview (Still NKJV)

"And she will bring forth a Son, and you shall call His name Jesus, for He will save His people from their sins." So all this was done that it might be fulfilled which was spoken by the Lord through the prophet, saying: "Behold, the virgin shall be with child, and bear a Son, and they shall call His name Immanuel," which is translated, "God with us." (Mt 1:21-23)

Therefore the Lord Himself will give you a sign: Behold, the virgin shall conceive and bear a Son, and shall call His name Immanuel. (Isa 7:14)

Yes, I know. Those verses were included together in the first

section of Shh – Prayer in Progress – In Love. But they are so beautiful

they deserve display in both sections.

You have heard that it was said, *'You shall love your neighbor* and hate your enemy.' But I say to you, love your enemies, bless those who curse you, do good to those who hate you, and pray for those who spitefully use you and persecute you, that you may be sons of your Father in heaven; for He makes His sun rise on the evil and on the good, and sends rain on the just and on the unjust. For if you love those who love you, what reward have you? Do not even the tax collectors do the same? And if you greet your brethren only, what do you do more *than others?* Do not even the tax collectors do so? Therefore you shall be perfect, just as your Father in heaven is perfect. (Mt 5:43-48)

Jesus said to him, "*'You shall love the LORD your God with all your heart, with all your soul, and with all your mind.'* This is *the* first and great commandment. And *the* second *is* like it. *'You shall love your neighbor as yourself.'* On these two commandments hang all the Law and the Prophets." (Mt 22:37-40)

Lord, some people might think it just a "coincidence" that the Bible so often says to love God so, so much - but we need to focus on that, don't we? I know You keep telling us that for a reason. And I know Your reason should be important to us. It is important for us, right?

> Jesus answered him, "The first of all the commandments is: *'Hear, O Israel, the Lord our God, the Lord is one. And you shall love the LORD your God with all your heart, with all your soul, with all your mind, and with all your strength.'* This is the first commandment. And the second, like it, is this: *'You shall love your neighbor as yourself.'* There is no other commandment greater than these."

> So the scribe said to Him, "Well said, Teacher. You have spoken the truth, for there is one God, and there is no other but He. And to love Him with all the heart, with all the understanding, with all the soul, and with all the strength, and to love one's neighbor as oneself, is more than all the whole burnt offerings and sacrifices." Now when Jesus saw that he answered wisely, He said to him, "You are not far from the kingdom of God." But after that no one dared question Him. (Mk 12:29-34)

> Then Pilate said to Him, "Do You not hear how many things they testify against You?" But He answered him not one word, so that the governor marvelled greatly. Mk 27:13-14

> He was oppressed and He was afflicted,
> Yet He opened not His mouth;
> He was led as a lamb to the slaughter,
> And as a sheep before its shearers is silent,
> So He opened not His mouth. (Isa 53:7)

Having already been reported in the Old Testament section of these secret love notes, these words are not reported again in this section because they are pretty. They are reported because Jesus did not speak, and in *not speaking* He tells us He loves us so, so much. Because He did not speak although He could have called a hundred thousand angels to free Him. Now we can have the spiritual power and discernment through His Holy Spirit, to speak up for Him. How can we not love Him so, so much?

> Then they spat on Him, and took the reed and struck Him on the head. And when they had mocked Him, they took the robe off Him, put His *own* clothes on Him, and led Him away to be crucified. (Mat 27:30-31)

> I gave My back to those who struck *Me*,
> And my cheeks to those who plucked out the beard;
> I did not hide My face from shame and spitting. (Isa 53-7)

And certainly those words are not repeated in this section because they are pretty. They are a graphic description of just a little bit of the horror our Lord endured because He loved us "a lotta bit."

> But I say to you who hear: Love your enemies, do good to those who hate you, bless those who curse you, and pray for those who spitefully use you. To him who strikes you on *one* cheek, offer the other also. And from him who takes away your cloak, do not withhold *your* tunic either. Give to everyone who asks of you. And from him who takes away your goods, do not ask *them* back.

And just as you want men to do to you, you also do to them likewise.

But if you love those who love you, what credit is that to you? For even sinners love those who love them. And if you do good to those who do good to you, what credit is that to you? For even sinners do the same. And if you lend *to those* from whom you hope to receive back, what credit is that to you? For even sinners lend to sinners to receive as much back. But love your enemies, do good, and lend, hoping for nothing in return; and your reward will be great, and you will be sons of the Most High. For He is kind to the unthankful and evil. Therefore be merciful, just as your Father also is merciful. (Lk 6:27-36)

And Jesus answered and said to him, "Simon, I have something to say to you."
So he said, "Teacher, say it."
"There was a certain creditor who had two debtors. One owed five hundred denarii, and the other fifty. And when they had nothing with which to repay, he freely forgave them both. Tell Me, therefore, which of them will love him more?"
Simon answered and said, "I suppose the *one* whom he forgave more."
And He said to him, "You have rightly judged." Then He turned to the woman and said to Simon, "Do you see this woman? I entered your house; you gave me no water for my feet, but she has washed My feet with her tears and wiped *them* with the hair of her head. You gave Me no kiss, but this woman has not ceased to kiss My feet since the time I came in. You did not anoint My head with oil, but this woman has anointed my feet with fragrant oil.
Therefore I say to you, her sins, *which are* many, are forgiven, for she loved much. But to whom little is forgiven, *the same* loves little."
Then He said to her, "Your sins are forgiven."
And those who sat at the table with Him began to say to themselves, "Who is this who even forgives sins?"
Then He said to the woman, "Your faith has saved you. Go in peace." (Lk 7:40-50)

Oh Father, oh Lord Jesus, oh Holy Spirit, Luke 7:40-50 says so much. Even the numbers 7:40-50 seem beautiful, attracting my attention for me to remember. We looked at some of those verses earlier, but they deserve another visit. It seems to me anyone who has been saved would have to have an enormous appreciation for those verses. I know I do. And I resolve to try to let them help guide me. Thank you for them.

> And behold, a certain lawyer stood up and tested Him, saying, Teacher, what shall I do to inherit eternal life?"
>
> He said to him, "What is written in the law?" What is your reading of it?"
>
> So he answered and said, " *'You shall love the LORD your God with all your heart, with all your soul, with all your strength, and with all your mind,'* and *'your neighbor as yourself.'"* And He said to him, "You have answered rightly; do this and you will live." (Lk 10:25-28)

Father, I see what just happened there. The lawyer asked an important question. "Teacher, what shall I do to inherit eternal life?" But he was just trying to trip Jesus up. He seemed a good enough guy, but as we will soon see in verse 29, with another question, the lawyer was trying to justify himself.

Grace was not yet on the throne. It was not time for Jesus to get into an open discussion with a lawyer to answer the first question by proclaiming the Gospel. What did Jesus do? He did something indicative of Godly wisdom under the circumstances. He asked the man to answer his own question, and the way he said it, restricted the lawyer's answer to the law, staying away from the ultimate answer of grace. Yet we know the law cannot save man. Only the grace of God can. Yet Jesus began His answer to the question about eternal life by saying, "What is written in the law? What is your reading of it?"

Nobody ever tripped Jesus up. The man then told Jesus that the way to inherit eternal life is to obey the greatest and second greatest commandments. That might get the man an "A" with God grading on the curve, at that time, but it would not get him an "A+" today, and You do not grade on the curve. Yet, Jesus told him he was right, if he would do that he would live.

I find it interesting that Jesus was very nice to him and, in effect, Jesus seemed to compliment him on knowing the right answer. Somehow, with divine wisdom, Jesus had gone from the one being interrogated, to the position of being the one grading the lawyer's answer.

But what really happened there? In His answer, Jesus was avoiding opening up the discussion with a lawyer, publicly, before being

220

crucified, the plan of salvation. The law could not save; otherwise Jesus would not have had to bear our sins on the cross. What Jesus refrained from elaborating about was that we cannot "...love the LORD your God with all your heart, with all your soul, with all your strength, and with all your mind, 'and' your neighbor as yourself..." on our own. Plus, and this is a 'biggie,' even if we could love God that much on our own, which we cannot without a savior, the sins we committed before we loved God that much would still condemn us, because "all have sinned and come short of the glory of God." In the Old Testament, people were saved by grace, by believing God about the coming of the Christ. But the day of this lawyer's question, with the atmosphere of the scene, was not the time or place for public revelations of the unprecedented glory that would soon take place in the death, burial, and resurrection of the Lord Jesus Christ, and a new beginning for all mankind.

So when Jesus said, do that (love God that much) and you will live, it was couched in Jesus' knowledge that the only way the man could love that much would be with a prerequisite - a knowledge of Christ. Therefore, if the man loved God that much, just as Jesus said, the man would live.

The Bible tells us over and over, in many ways, that to be saved we only have to believe and accept the gift from God. That is a less difficult entrance requirement than loving God with all our heart, soul, strength, and mind. Hence Jesus just went along with the lawyer and said, yes, if you do all that, you will pass. And certainly that is true. But we cannot get there from here. On the road to heaven, before we can absorb that much love from God, to return it to Him, we have to go to the first traffic light and accept Jesus as our savior. The road to heaven is a toll road. The price is Jesus' blood, and only the price of Jesus' blood pays the price for us to pass.

> But he, wanting to justify himself, said to Jesus, "And who is my neighbor?"
> Then Jesus answered and said: "A certain *man* went down from Jerusalem to Jericho, and fell among thieves, who stripped him of his clothing, wounded *him* and departed, leaving *him* half dead. Now by chance a certain priest came down that road. And when he saw him, he passed by on the other side. Likewise a Levite, when he arrived at that place, came and looked, and passed by on the other side. But a certain Samaritan, as he journeyed, came where he was. And when he saw him, he had compassion. So he went to *him* and bandaged his wounds, pouring on oil and wine; and he set him on his own animal, brought him to an inn, and took care of him. On the next day, when he departed, he took out two denarii, gave *them* to the innkeeper, and said to him, 'Take care of him; and whatever more you spend, when I come again, I will repay you. So which of these three do you think was neighbor to him who fell among the thieves?"
> And he said, "He who showed mercy on him."
> Then Jesus said to him, "Go and do likewise." (Lk 10:29-37)

But people get it backwards. The secular world can understand the standard of being a good Samaritan. But here is another place where Dr. Charles Stanley might say "Listen". The secular world does not understand loving God. People need to know about and focus on the Greatest Commandment. Sometimes maybe you do have to start with the second greatest. Sometimes that is needed in order to soften hardened hearts, starting with something they can relate to, with them having seen love in others. But starting with only the second greatest invites *ignoreance* of the Greatest Commandment and invites never addressing it. To reflect obeying the Greatest Commandment, you need to give it the publicity it deserves. Loving God is like a brand name for commandments. Brand name recognition is important in the spiritual world. *Loving God is the Greatest product.* It should have a more recognizable brand name. If you don't talk about your love for God, how are you going to be a good example and open up a door that encourages others to give publicity to the brand name? Down the road that also leads to why you love God, which brings out the name of Jesus.

> For God so loved the world that He gave His only begotten Son, that whoever believes in Him should not perish but have everlasting life. (Jn 3:16)

Think this way: Greatest Commandment deserves better Brand Name recognition.

"I do not receive honor from men. But I know you, that you do not have the love of God in you. I have come in My Father's name, and you do not receive Me; if another comes in his own name, him you will receive. How can you believe, who receive honor from one another, and do not seek the honor that *comes* from the only God? Do not think that I shall accuse you to the Father; there is *one* who accuses you—Moses, in whom you trust. For if you believed Moses, you would believe Me; for he wrote about Me. But if you do not believe his writings, how will you believe My words?" (Jn 5:41-47)

"I am the good shepherd. The good shepherd gives His life for the sheep. (Jn 10:11)

He will feed His flock like a shepherd;
He will gather the lambs with His arm,
And carry *them* in His bosom,
And gently lead those who are with young. (Isa 40:11)

Father, how wonderful, how marvelous, that we have the Good

Shepherd to love, and to follow.

"...A new commandment I give to you, that you love one another; as I have loved you, that you also love one another. By this all will know that you are my disciples, if you have love for one another." (Jn 13:34-35)

This is My commandment, that you love one another as I have loved you. Greater love has no one than this, than to lay down one's life for his friends. You are My friends if you do whatever I command you. No longer do I call you servants, for a servant does not know what his master is doing; but I have called you friends, for all things that I heard from My Father I have made known to you. You did not choose Me, but I chose you and appointed you that you should go and bear fruit, and *that* your fruit should remain, that whatever you ask the Father in My name He may give you. These things I command you, that you love one another. (Jn 15:12-17)

Then she ran and came to Simon Peter, and to the other disciple, whom Jesus loved, and said to them, "They have taken away the Lord out of the tomb, and we do not know where they have laid Him." (Jn 20:2)

I think love and humor, like love and marriage, "go together like a horse and carriage." And since 1 John 4:8 says "God is love," I just have to believe You enjoy goodness in humor. In John 20:2, John refers to himself as "...the other disciple, whom Jesus loved..." and that seems so funny to me.

John withheld his own name since John's spiritual gift was mercy (love), and love is not self-seeking. But John found a way to enjoy, and to speak with a truthful tongue-in-cheek in his writing, subtly publicizing the delight that Jesus loved him.

Peter therefore went out, and the other disciple, and were going to the tomb. So they both ran together, and the other disciple outran Peter and came to the tomb first. (Jn 20:3-4)

In Jn 20:3-4, John still withheld his name. But love none the less has victory with the tongue-in-cheek writer again, in good humor camaraderie, in the inerrant Word of God, inspired by You, God, writing, "…and the other disciple outran Peter…."

Listen, there is no newsworthy or historical importance to one disciple (John) outrunning the other (Peter). And what a coincidence that John would tell of such an unimportant happening anyway, in the Bible - in the Bible, at the time he arrived at the scene of the resurrection, the single most important event in history.

God, do You have bad timing? Never. Do You not understand what is important? Certainly You do. Man needs to know God understands *everything*. That is important. Francie's Tennessee Temple poem, in Chapter One made that crystal clear.

The purpose of Your words written by John there, in the inerrant Word of God, inspired by God, is found in John's spiritual gift, love. Love and good humor really do go together like a horse and carriage. And God, You give each of us our own distinct personality. And You want us to use what You give us. Even in the Holy Bible.

Jesus showed that He loved good humor. His stories, told with loving humor, in the culture of that time, were well understood and well received by the good-spirited people to whom He spoke. And humor is throughout the Bible. It starts in Genesis. I can just imagine Your restrained chuckle as Adam says, "The woman that You gave me made me do it." (Paraphrase of Genesis 3:8-12).

How easily we miss the humor when we are not looking for it. Adam is blaming You and Eve in the same breath. Man blames everybody except himself.

But the ladies shouldn't get too smug, because in the very next verse, Eve tells You the serpent made her do it. At least she did not blame You.

All of this is written seriously, because life and death is a serious matter. But it is written in a good humor way. Good humor expedites learning, and it expedites receiving from God. It is a badge of love that opens the *gate* to our heart and quickens the *gait* of our minds. If you are not looking for it, it can be hard to see the smile on the face of the writer, whether it be a writer of thousands of years ago, or one sitting "write here, write now"

Looking for Easter eggs hidden by God is fun for His children. Finding them is marvelous fun! Maybe the humor with John would not be so obvious to baby Christians. But sometimes the Father leaves humor, like Easter eggs, just lying on top of the grass so even His youngest children can find them.

Back to the first book of the Bible now, to see Abraham again. Some people do not laugh at anything. Some are already "good humor folks" and will laugh at the drop of an Easter egg, uh…at the drop of a hat. Anyway, now we go to two Easter eggs in one, and we are still in Genesis, the first book of the Bible. God loves good humor.

Before we travel back to Genesis again though, Lord, I recently learned laughing extends your life. I mean, not Your life, but it will extend the lives of readers. Yes sir, extends their lives! Scientists have known that for years - though not nearly as many years as have You. From the web site of HELPGUIDE.org, here are some important words, "When laughter is shared, it binds people together and increases happiness and intimacy. In addition to the domino effect of joy and amusement, laughter also triggers healthy physical changes in the body. Humor and laughter strengthen your immune system, boost your energy, diminish pain, and protect you from the damaging effects of stress. Best of all, this priceless medicine is fun, free, and easy to use."

Hmm, maybe laughter can help with leukemia? Hey, have you heard the one about…no, not now…let's go back to Genesis, where Abraham and Sarah said to themselves, "God makes me laugh!" Would God Almighty really do such a thing? And if He did, would He put it in His Book, where God and everybody could see it? And guess what I learned. The name "Isaac" means "laughter." Isaac is also the name of the son You gave Abraham in his old age. Abraham was a hundred years old, and Sarah was just about ten years younger. I am reminded that as I write this page I'm only seventy and Francie is fourteen years younger, but I don't think Francie would think that was so funny. So I won't. But the moral of this story may also be, "God always gets the last laugh." But I know You want us to laugh, and be in good humor. That's life. And You said to choose life.

Okay, here are some more Easter eggs, and You did just put these on top of the grass, where they would be easy to find. In Genesis 17:16-17, You made Abraham laugh. Good humor abounds.

> "And I will bless her and also give you a son by her; then I will bless her, and she shall be a *mother of* nations; kings of peoples shall be from her."
> Then Abraham fell on his face and laughed, and said in his heart, "Shall a *child* be born to a man who is one hundred years old? And shall Sarah, who is ninety years old, bear a *child*?"

That's what it said, Abraham fell down laughing. And it wasn't just Abraham that laughed. Sarah overheard You and Abraham talking and she laughed, only she didn't fall down laughing out loud like Abraham did. She only laughed inside herself - and You heard her! She denied it, but you can't fool God, even when He is having fun with you. Then in Genesis 18:13-15 we hear:

> And the Lord said to Abraham, "Why did Sarah laugh, saying, 'Shall I surely bear a *child*, since I am old?' Is anything too hard for the Lord? At the appointed time I will return to you, according to the time of life, and Sarah shall have a son."
> But Sarah denied *it*, saying, "I did not laugh," for she was afraid. And He said, "No, but you did laugh!"

Lord, I say You were smiling a big smile when You said that. What do you say? As we know, God, You did get the last laugh. You always do. Most people just can't see Your good humor. Thank You for undeserved blessings You bestow on us. Thank You for Your love. Thank You for your Your mercy and Your amazing grace. Thank You for Easter eggs for us to find.

> So when they had eaten breakfast, Jesus said to Simon Peter, "Simon, *son* of Jonah, do you love Me more than these?"
> He said to Him, "Yes, Lord; You know that I love You."
> He said to him, "Feed My lambs."
> He said to him again a second time, "Simon, *son* of Jonah, do you love Me?"

He said to Him, "Yes, Lord; You know that I love You."
He said to him, "Tend my sheep."
He said to him the third time, "Simon, *son* of Jonah, do you love
Me?" Peter was grieved because He said to him the third time,
"Do you love Me?"
And he said to Him, "Lord, You know all things; You know that I
love You."
Jesus said to him, "Feed my sheep." (Jn 21:15-17)

Lord, I think readers should review the Chapter Two exhibit, "Shepherd in Sheep's Clothing" by Bob Ivey. Secondarily, I would like to show them a tiny Easter egg. I always thought Jesus gave the same instruction three times in the above verses. But in writing this I notice He did not. He said, 1. Feed My Lambs, 2. Tend My Sheep, and 3. Feed My Sheep. I checked deeper and the KJV had said "feed" all three times. The NKJV says "tend" the second time. I checked with a linguistics expert, my son, Jon-Michael, and I am believing the NKJV is more precise. Jon-Michael says the second time the original language is just a little more than actually feeding, but the difference could simply include leading to a pasture rather than literally feeding.

What is the significance? I don't know. I can see feeding the little lambs first. They come first with Jesus. They can't take care of themselves. And, thinking about it, maybe the sheep need tending before feeding. Maybe Jesus saw sheep having more urgent needs to be tended to

than being fed. And finally, the sheep need to be fed. Significant?
Every word out of the mouth of God is significant. And that, I would say
to my dear grandchildren, and dear grand nieces and nephews, may in fact
be why Jesus befuddled Simon Peter, so you and I could find this little
Easter egg together. Yep, this one is for the little lambs that Jesus loves so
much! What do you think? Think about it. The feeding would relate to
feeding God's Word, right? Maybe the sheep need to be led to different
pastures before they are fed? Could that be it? What do you think? Maybe
since each question dealt with loving Jesus, the key is Jesus' sheep are
completely trusting and dependent on the love from the shepherd they
follow?

> What then shall we say to these things? If God *is* for us, who *can
> be* against us? He who did not spare His own Son, but delivered
> Him up for us all, how shall He not with Him also freely give us
> all things? Who shall bring a charge against God's elect? *It is* God
> who justifies. Who *is* he who condemns? *It is* Christ who dies, and
> furthermore is also risen, who is even at the right hand of God,
> who makes intercession for us. Who shall separate us from the
> love of Christ? *Shall* tribulation, or distress, or persecution, or
> famine, or nakedness, or peril, or sword? As it is written:
>
> > *"For Your sake we are killed all day long;*
> > *We are accounted as sheep for the slaughter."*
>
> Yet in all these things we are more than conquerors through Him
> who loved us. For I am persuaded that neither death nor life, nor
> angels nor principalities nor powers, nor things present nor things
> to come, nor height nor depth, nor any other created thing, shall be

232

able to separate us from the love of God which is in Christ Jesus our Lord. (Ro 8:31-39)

Let no debt remain outstanding, except the continuing debt to love one another, for he who loves his fellowman has fulfilled the law. The commandments, "Do not commit adultery," "Do not murder," "Do not steal," "Do not covet," and whatever other commandment there may be, are summed up in this one rule: "Love your neighbor as yourself." Love does no harm to its neighbor. Therefore love is the fulfillment of the law. (Ro 13:8-10)

I particularly enjoyed in Chapter 3: Love is the Principal Principle, writing about the purpose of the rule being to guide us to use the principle, yet the principle of love rules over any rule, and quoting Spurgeon: "...for it is written, 'God is love,' which is an alias for grace.... I say, then, that grace is enthroned by conquest, by right, and by power..."

For the love of Christ compels us, because we judge thus: that if One died for all, then all died; and He died for all, that those who live should live no longer for themselves, but for Him who died for them and rose again. Therefore, from now on, we regard no one according to the flesh. Even though we have known Christ according to the flesh, yet now we know *Him thus* no longer. Therefore, if anyone *is* in Christ, *he is* a new creation; old things have passed away; behold, all things have become new. Now all things *are* of God, who has reconciled us to Himself through Jesus Christ, and has given us the ministry of reconciliation, that is, that God was in Christ reconciling the world to Himself, not imputing their trespasses to them, and has committed to us the word of reconciliation. (2 Co 5:14-19)

Finally, brethren, farewell. Become complete. Be of good comfort, be of one mind, live in peace; and the God of love and peace will be with you. (2 Co 13:11)

But the fruit of the Spirit is love, joy, peace, longsuffering, kindness, goodness, faithfulness, gentleness, self-control. Against such there is no law. (Gal 5:22)

Peace to the brethren, and love with faith, from God the Father and the Lord Jesus Christ. Grace *be* with all those who love our Lord Jesus Christ in sincerity. Amen. (Eph 6:23-24)

Therefore if *there is* any consolation in Christ, if any comfort of love, if any fellowship of the Spirit, if any affection and mercy, fulfill my joy by being like-minded, having the same love, *being* of one accord, of one mind. *Let* nothing *be done* through selfish ambition or conceit, but in lowliness of mind let each esteem others better than himself. Let each of you look out not only for his own interests, but also for the interests of others. (Ph 2:1-4)

For God has not given us a spirit of fear, but of power and of love and of a sound mind. (2 Ti 1:7)

And let us consider one another in order to stir up love and good works, not forsaking the assembling of ourselves together, as *is* the manner of some, but exhorting *one another*, and so much the more as you see the Day approaching. (He 10:24-25)

Let brotherly love continue. Do not forget to entertain strangers, for by so doing some have unwittingly entertained angels. Remember the prisoners as if chained with them - those who are mistreated - since you yourselves are in the body also. (He 13:1-3)

Father, if folks are like me, there are a lot of things we know but

we need reminders about. One, we should pray for anyone You might be

bringing to our attention. Who knows, sometime, somewhere, somehow,

when we least expect it, the right combination of seeds, and fertilizer, and water, might cause germination, and the person we thought would be lost forever is found, by the grace of God.

Here is an example. You sacrificed Your Son on the cross. How much of a sacrifice would it be for us, for us to silently pray and just say a code word like, "Sarah" to expedite quick prayer? I'll explain about Sarah.

On the prison trips, I started a practice of praying for anybody who caught my attention - in restaurants, wherever, it didn't matter. Anyone I would see, I would silently pray for them to be saved, and if already saved, to be drawn closer to the Lord. That is not so easy when multiple people are in sight. So I shortened it to my eyes focusing quickly on each one of them and quickly for each one, silently, saying, "Saved and closer," with the understanding that the Lord would excuse my shorthand. Then with huge groups, for each person I could see, I would say, "Sarah," because I could say Sarah more quickly than I could say saved and closer, and the Lord would still know what the code meant. Why Sarah? Sarah starts with the same two letters as does "saved and." And Sarah starts with the same two as does just, "saved," also. Coincidentallly, she was the wife of the one called, "the father of faith."

And God, You said she would be "the mother of many nations." And secret codes, like inside jokes that only family members know why they are funny, secret codes bind people together. We know God is three persons, and Jesus is the "tie that binds" for us. So "Sarah" to all who read this.

Over a period of time, and not in this sequence, I heard, "Don't just say, 'Que sera sera, whatever will be, will be.' Instead, say, 'Sarah' or 'Saved and closer.' If there is time, say something like the following."

Father, that person that my eyes are focused on, I thank You for bringing to my attention that person. I don't know that person's spiritual condition, only You do. You know everything, and that is wonder-full. I pray now that if that person is not saved, that You would, somehow, somewhere, sometime, some way, save that person. If that person is saved, I pray you would draw that person nearer to you. Thank You, for answering this prayer. In the precious Holy name of the Lord Jesus Christ I pray. Amen.

The above, Father, is the message I believe you wanted me to deliver. However, expressions using words like *wonder-full*, are simply a reflection of my personality, and not necessarily words that You would ever use in communication.

For me, usually, "Saved and closer" becomes the more frequent prayer of the three, focusing on someone in particular in a "Be His sheep" way. What? You know, we are to each be a sheep of the omniscient

Shepherd. I wouldn't do that kind of praying if I didn't think You wanted me to. Maybe some people might say it is a waste of time, and of focus. Maybe. But maybe it is the most important thing we can ever do in our entire lives. I think, that at the worst, it will only draw the one praying closer to the Lord. So at the worst it would be a blessing.

"At the worst?" Draw me closer to the Lord? Oh NO. Please – please - don't throw me in dat dere briar patch. "Re-born and bred in da briar patch, re-born and bred in da briar patch." Did Brer' Rabbit hide Easter eggs for his children to find? I don't think so. He wasn't real. And yet he brought joy to children all over our nation. God is real. And God does *hide* spiritual Easter eggs for His children to find. And that joy thrills them.

Some might even say the finding of Easter eggs hidden by God for His adult children can bring rejoicing inside them that might even make them sound silly. Well, there is a silly poem that I have always liked because my name is William and the title of the poem is "You Are Old Father William," written by Lewis Carroll more than a hundred years ago. I just happened to run across it again recently. But in the interest of moving on, I will say this instead: Here are some Easter Egg Candidates.

LEWIS CARROLL AND C. S. LEWIS:

Was Lewis Carroll's middle initial S.? No, he didn't have one. But C. S. Lewis did, and it was C. S. Lewis who said, "It is in the process of being worshiped that God communicates His presence to men." Not sure C. S. Lewis was right? Test it. Now. Peace, be still.

Actually, Lewis Carroll was not Lewis Carroll's real name, it was a pen name, and Lewis Carroll died the year C. S. Lewis was born. Is that fact a coincidence, or is that coincidence a distraction? They were both extraordinary writers. More than spectacular even. And maybe there is an Easter egg in there somewhere, just for you. Where is it? You'll have to look for it yourself. It is in the process of being looked for that the Easter egg's bright colors communicate its presence to God's children.

When I said, "It is in the process of being looked for that the Easter egg's bright colors communicate its presence to God's children – I was hoping to trigger in the minds of adult children the thought of going back and focusing on the ramifications of C. S. Lewis' statement, "It is in the process of being worshiped that God communicates His presence to men." It is an Easter egg because it is a bright and shinning spiritual gem. Worship God now, and seek communication of the presence of Love.

In order to hear the still small voice within, first, be still. If you are too busy to listen, you are too busy for life and peace, joy and hope. Work ethic is in the other direction for awhile.

Lord, here are some things all of your children need to hear:

Put God first, and do it with thanksgiving, and His glory brightens the way for you. All blessings flow from God, not 86% or even 93%, but all! Get up close to Him so you can hear them coming. As Red Skelton might say about here, "Here comes a flock of 'um now."

If it is not a blessing from Him, it is not a blessing. When laughter is a blessing, it is a blessing from Whom?

Oh, so maybe laughter can be from God? Smile and the whole world smiles with you. Laugh with God, and the whole world scratches its head. (God is fun. "With God all things are possible." Matthew 19:26)

God was so funny when, like God knew he would do, Abraham fell down laughing, and we are still trying to figure out how those two had such a good-humor relationship. With faith, it is possible to please God.

Could faith and good humor go together like love and marriage? Without faith it is impossible to tell a good-humor joke with confidence.

But really now, does God laugh? All I can tell people is, it is no coincidence that, "Ho! Ho! Ho!" and "Merry Christmas" go together like love and marriage. It is just that "Love" is not self-seeking, so God hides behind a big red suit to spread the Word, It is now a throne of Grace.

Little children sit in His lap at the throne of Grace. They experience a hint of the joy of His giving nature. Seeds of His love are sown. His Spirit tells adult children, "If you will remember how and why it became a throne of Grace, you can come closer to the great joy of loving with all your heart."

> In this you greatly rejoice, though now for a little while, if need be, you have been grieved by various trials, that the genuineness of your faith, being much more precious than gold that perishes, though it is tested by fire, may be found to praise, honor, and glory at the revelation of Jesus Christ, whom having not seen you love. Though now you do not see Him, yet believing, you rejoice with joy inexpressible and full of glory, receiving the end of your faith--the salvation of your souls. 1 Pe 1:6-9

If it is useful to pray for someone to be healed physically, why would it not be useful to pray for someone to be saved, and for someone to be drawn closer to the Lord? How glorious would it be to have such prayers honored by omnipotent Almighty God? How glorious would it be, for the Lord Jesus Christ, for great numbers of people to be saved or drawn closer to the Lord? How glorious would it be for great numbers to pray for others to be saved and if already saved, to be drawn closer to the Lord? How glorious would it be for our nation to thereby turn back to the Lord!

You can even do it sitting on the sofa watching a football game. But when the commercial came on, and I found myself starting to pray, "saved and closer," as I focused on each of two cartoon characters in a show being advertised, I caught myself, and realized I need to remind myself that the prayers need to be in spirit and in truth, for real souls, earnestly, and it was serious business that needed to quickly keep focus on the Lord and at the same time heartfelt concern for each precious soul.

In this phase our job is to do the praying. The rest of the job is God's. There is zero pressure for us. We just do the job we are called to do. And it is a very easy job. But it requires caring about strangers, with a heart that wants to obey God and to help others.

That reminds me of the true story of decades ago, of an Atlanta Hawks player. I'll call him Bill, so as not to risk insulting anyone without insulting myself. The coach said during practice, "Bill, you have got to start getting more rebounds!" The player responded, "But coach, I don't have a *history* of getting more rebounds." You don't have a history of praying for salvation decisions? That is reason not to do it?

Father, I know this book is about love, but that is the point, because hell is real. Jesus said it is, and He said the only way out is through Him, while we are still on earth. While I don't want to offend my friends who are not Christians, and I have Jewish friends and clients, and agnostic and atheist friends and clients, they should care that I care about them, rather than be offended by my words. If they were in a building that was on fire, maybe they wouldn't want me to drag them out, but I would at least insist on putting a ladder up to the window so they could make an educated choice. Readers, I hope you would too - even though you may not even know them. So think about joining me with, "saved and closer," and *Sarah*. Pastors, youth ministers, speakers at Fellowship of Christian Athletes meetings, and everyone else whom God loves is invited to pick up the *Sarah* banner and run with it. "And that's including YOU!"

As a reminder, I prayed for my mother's salvation, as did others. I say God answered those prayers and He would love to respond to *Sarah* prayers from people everywhere. Remember how Mother was saved? Wanda Pyant had a nurse's degree, and could have taken a job earning more money, but she came to work for us and stayed with us for years, at the same lower pay scale that the other caregivers received. Was it a coincidence that the right person, with the right heart, with a Bible was in the right place at the right time for Emily Barnes Ivey? No. And it happened the morning Daddy passed away, without Mother knowing he had, and it was just four months before she passed away. If we do not practice "saved and closer" prayers, for even strangers we see, what will we say if God asks us, "Why did you not pray for them? Yours was the easy part." What shall we answer to Him for souls really and truly going to hell, "Sorry, but you see, Lord, I had this thing called 'inertia' so obviously I couldn't do it. I don't have a history of praying for strangers to be saved."

Do you love Jesus just a litta bit? Let your answer guide your actions.

Now let's talk about a different Sarah, and God's Good Humor:

Most of what we read about God is from another time and another culture. And also some things can only be discerned spiritually. So like we might not catch on to God's good humor, some young folks who don't know the popular songs from "the good old days" might not grasp the meaning of what us older guys might say. We might say, "Back then we had a horse named Sarah, but we had to get rid of her." Why is that? "Because Serenade in the Night." (A beautiful song.) Now I didn't say it was a good joke, but it is something told in good humor. And good humor is what I am attempting to convey a message about. God is love. Love loves to radiate good humor.

We err in not seeing the good humor, because we don't relate to the spirit in the language of the era, because the language seems stiff and foreign to us. And again, it is just plain hard to see the smile of love on the face of the writer from centuries gone by. Also, our society has learned about God from Hollywood and the media, who certainly have done a less than wonderful job of reporting the greatest love story ever lived. So to rise above all that, we need to just go to the Source, and the instruments the Source uses. Which is to say, read the Bible daily, associate with folks who do the same, because fellowship educates as the Lord speaks through others, and talk to the Lord directly, much more often than daily. Continuously is the ultimate standard.

Here is an old one. Johnny's teacher asked him to tell the class the difference between agnostic and apathy. He responded, "I don't know, and I don't care!"

If we really knew God, we would really care about God. He knows everything, and still He cared about you and me so much to be crucified for us. Before Hallmark was, He cared enough to send the very best, Jesus.

Whoever does not love does not know God, because God is love. (1 Jn 4:8)

To know Him is to love Him, because, to know Him is to know love. (Just me? Or Him through me?)

> No one has seen God at any time. If we love one another, God abides in us, and His love has been perfected in us. By this we know that we abide in Him, and He in us, because He has given us of His Spirit. And we have seen and testify that the Father has sent the Son as Savior of the world. Whoever confesses that Jesus is the Son of God, God abides in him, and he in God. And we have known and believed the love that God has for us. God is love, and he who abides in love abides in God, and God in him. (1 Jn4:12-16)

Verse 15 above is so clear. "Whoever confesses that Jesus is the Son of God, God abides in him, and he in God." Readers, I hope I can say, from Robyn's Christmas poem, "And that's including YOU!" He loves you regardless, but have you confessed that Jesus is the Son of God? If not, why not set things right, with God right now?

> Love has been perfected among us in this: that we may have boldness in the day of judgment; because as He is, so are we in this world. There is no fear in love; but perfect love casts out fear, because fear involves torment. But he who fears has not been made perfect in love. We love Him because He first loved us. (1 Jn 4:17-19)

> If perfect love casts out fear, that means we can be in good humor

with You, Lord, right? If fear is out, then good humor can come in, right? I am sure the answer is respectfully, yes.

Lord when we are in good humor, close to You, I suspect You inhabit our laughter, just as the Bible says You inhabit our praise. That's just a suspicion I have. Readers, check it out for yourselves. Next time you are in good humor, close to Him, and laughing, notice do you feel His presence? You have to look for it. Think about Him being in your presence as you laugh, I hope you will suspect, "When you laugh, in good humor, the Lord your God laughs with you." Give it a test run.

Laugh, you're on eternal camera. Laugh, God needs a good one for you. Laugh, it is good for your health. Laugh, we have met the Victor, and He is ours! If you can't laugh, just smile, and say, "He haw, he haw, he haw," remembering you are not a donkey and still He wants to talk to and through you. Pat your head while rubbing your stomach, while listening to the still small voice, and keeping your eye on the big picture, His grace. You might hear, "I love you!"

> If someone says, "I love God," and hates his brother, he is a liar; for he who does not love his brother whom he has seen, how can he love God whom he has not seen? And this commandment we have from Him: that he who loves God *must* love his brother also. (1 Jn 4:20-21)

Father, I am about to step away for a moment, to ask a question of others. Readers, do you pray for your brothers and sisters in Christ? I am about to pray for the good health of every person who will read this book. I can't do that by name, of course, but God already knows who you are. And, given that I would like my leukemia to stay in remission, I covet your prayers. So, I ask that you also pray now, that every person in Christ who reads this book receive good health. I certainly am a reader of this book, so your prayer would equally include me. I would also like for us to pray for our nation to return to the Lord. And stay with the Lord. My observation is that God likes to honor prayer in volumes, and all of us praying for each other this way could speak volumes to the Lord. If you would sacrifice your time and the full attention of your heart, to do such a thing, I expect God would appreciate it. I know I would. I expect I will pray for you again from time to time, as the Lord reminds me. Initially, I plan to do that on the first day of each month.

Father, thank you for the years of good health you have given me to live here on earth. You are the Creator and the Sustainer of life. I love You, and I love everything You represent. In Your goodness You have first loved me. And for me, You have even provided eternal life. That is an enormous thing. Words are not good enough to describe Your goodness nor great enough to describe Your greatness. Thank You that I know that nothing is impossible for You, and that I cannot over-estimate You.

Father, I come boldly before the throne of Grace, asking that ALL of Your children who read this book be given good health. I don't know what illnesses readers need cured, physical or emotional, but You do, and illness can be a hard burden, beyond instructiveness. I ask better than that for Your children. Their health and their lives are in Your hands. We choose to love You, and to accept the blessings You want us to be able to receive. You can also heal our land, and I ask that You bring the positive effects of Your love for us, leading us to love You like we have never done before, and let that then lead to the healing of our land, by You, through Your children. Let our hands and our hearts be Yours. Heal our land of corruption in high places and immorality in all places, as we return to the One who was crucified for us, and yet rose again. Father, lest I forget to thank You later, thank You now, for answering this prayer. I love you. In the name of my Lord Jesus Christ I pray. Amen.

God Is So Good.

The other day, Brother Tom told me about the telephone repairman who came to his house recently. The man finished up and told Brother Tom it was fixed. He could call out, but it would be about fifteen minutes before he would be able to receive calls. The man said he was going to leave, but he would call back in about twenty minutes to confirm it was working. Brother Tom lives near an interstate, and he said, "You mean you are going out on that expressway before confirming it? What if you get killed? When I die, I know I'm going to heaven. If you get killed today, do you know where you are going?" The man lowered his head and said, "Yes, I'm afraid I do. I'm going to hell." Brother Tom told him, "Well it doesn't have to be that way," and he led him to the Lord, right then and there. Brother Tom told me, "Bill, God is so good. I can't make the trips to prison with the guys to go fishing anymore, so the Lord brings the fish to me!" Pray that the Lord would lead to somebody like

Brother Tom, all the fish you pray for each day.

> As many as I love, I rebuke and chasten. Therefore be zealous and repent. Behold, I stand at the door and knock. If anyone hears My voice and opens the door, I will come in to him and dine with him, and he with Me. To him who overcomes I will grant to sit with Me on My throne, as I also overcame and sat down with My Father on His throne. (Re 3:19-21)
>
> Now I saw a new heaven and a new earth, for the first heaven and the first earth had passed away. Also there was no more sea. Then I, John, saw the holy city, New Jerusalem, coming down out of heaven from God, prepared as a bride adorned for her husband. And I heard a loud voice from heaven saying, "Behold, the tabernacle of God *is* with men, and He will dwell with them, and they shall be His people. God Himself will be with them *and be* their God. And God will wipe away every tear from their eyes; there shall be no more death, nor sorrow, nor crying. There shall be no more pain, for the former things have passed away."
>
> Then He who sat on the throne said, "Behold, I make all things new." And He said to me, "Write, for these words are true and faithful."
>
> And He said to me, "It is done! I am the Alpha and the Omega, the Beginning and the End. I will give of the fountain of the water of life freely to him who thirsts. He who overcomes shall inherit all things, and I will be his God and he shall be My son. (Re 21:1-7)

And the Lord said to me, in Almighty love:

> NOW AND FOR ETERNITY
> I AM the Throne of Grace
> I AM part of you
> I AM loving you

I am not defined by my love or lack thereof for God. I am not defined by whether or not I do what I should do, by whether or not I love God with all my heart, all my soul, all my strength, all my might, all my mind. I am defined by God's grace. That is exactly who I am. By God's grace, I am saved. Jesus came to save us, to give us life. We have to make a choice to accept or reject Him. Then He also came that we might have life more abundantly.

A Prayer God Would "Love" To Answer:

God wants you to love Him more. Why? Because the best thing you can do for yourself, is love Him more. God has given us some rules that are hard to follow. The most important of His rules for us - and the easiest to work on each day - is to love Him with all our heart by just loving Him more each day. Turn inertia into a helper rather than a hinderer.

Work with your inertia, consciously. Spend more time with God, and you will love Him more. You will want to spend more time with Him, and you will love Him more. On day one, maybe you can't love Him as much as you should. But decide to move toward that goal, one day at a time. Each day, ask Him to lead you in loving Him each day. If you are sincere, that is a prayer He would "love" to answer.

I want to follow the lead of two-year-old Robyn Ivey saying, "God thank you for giving me that song." In this case, "God, thank you for giving me this book." And, as the medical assistant at Georgia Cancer Specialists said, "I just thank the Lord He gave me the opportunity and the wisdom to do it." I think the most important part for me, or any of us, is in just trying to be a sheep of the omniscient Shepherd. And that is something we all can do, if we just will.

Good night dear grandchildren, and grandnieces and grandnephews. It is time to go to "sheep."

The secret *things belong* to the LORD our God, but those *things which are* revealed *belong* to us and to our children forever... . (Deuteronomy 29:29)

Chapter 16:

"T'was the Night *OF* Christmas"

I counted the book completed on December 25, made a copy, and took it to Brother Tom and Sister Maxine as a Christmas present, giving it to him Christmas night. The next day Brother Tom called and said he read every word of it, Christmas night, and it was the greatest Christmas present he ever received, but that I gave him too much credit. I'm telling you, I was thrilled. He and I have never had a disagreement, and we did not linger long on the subject of credit, but I could understand how he would feel in that situation, knowing that Jesus would deserve all the praise and all the glory. I would feel humbled by any, and still I am satisfied I did not give him too much credit.

For the prison trips, Brother Tom always gathered us together at the door of the van before we got in to go, and He prayed. He asked for souls to be saved, souls to come to a saving knowledge of the Lord Jesus Christ, and he always finished with, "and we will give You all the praise and all the glory." That is who Brother Tom is. Nothing describes him better than those last twelve words, "and we will give You all the praise and all the glory." He could not feel comfortable with anything less than that.

But lifting up Brother Tom is not taking away from the Lord. It just evidences how much more praise and glory the Lord is entitled to for raising up such a giant of a humble man. The Lord Jesus Christ deserves all the praise and all the glory, and I am convinced the Lord would consider me remiss if I did not point out right here and now, that I can hear seven words, from the future for Brother Tom, "Well done my good and faithful servant," and I have no doubt whatsoever that those words are from the Lord, and specifically addressed to Brother Tom and Sister Maxine. I have high hopes for their continued service and as an inspiration to so many people who have come to know the Lord - who have thereby come to KNOW LOVE because of that couple's walk with the Lord.

At prison, Brother Tom always insisted that we not try to convince anyone of anything. Tell them, yes, tell them, the good news, but try to convince them? No, that was the job of the Holy Spirit. We were to do our job and leave His job to Him. "Forget about the mule, load the wagon," was the expression. Plenty of people were ready to accept Jesus if we would just bring them the Word. The Holy Spirit works 24-7, and

He has so many just-right just-ready. In order to reach all who were ready, we had to forget about the mule. If the mule could be reached, it would have to be the convicting of the Holy Spirit that reached him first. No man can reach deeply into a hardened heart. The Holy Spirit can. So it was sow seeds for the mule, but move on quickly. Somebody else would be ready right now.

I can just hear Jesus now, putting the weak lambs first, telling Peter, "If you love me, feed my lambs."

Jesus is still with us today, telling us to feed his lambs, the weakest, to tend His sheep, those with great needs, and to feed His sheep. He is telling us to feed them with the Word of God, and tell them all about the throne of Grace, and about God's great love. He is telling us to tell them how much He wants what is best for them, and what is best for them is to love God like He loves them. And He is telling us to turn to the right and turn to the left, leading us down the right path at the right time, if we will just acknowledge Him so our love can grow. Love is not for keeping in a shoe box. Love is for growing, and growing, and growing, until you feel like you are just going to burst, and then you love as hard as you can for as long as you can. All the while you give, because love is for giving.

Like love, I reckon this book will never end. There is so much more I want to say. But if I don't close it sometime, no one else will ever be able to read what has been written so far. I know it seems strange for chapter sixteen to come after an *interlude*. But I feel led to do that. In the Bible, the number sixteen, my number in high school football, is the number most associated with - love. Love never ends.

But one more thing. Whenever I have spoken of Brother Tom, consider Sister Maxine included. The two are one. Sister Maxine went into the women's prisons, she graded the Bible lessons, she put little smiley face stickers here and there to brighten up the communication when she returned the graded lessons, she "stood by the stuff" as Brother Tom went out.

Yes, love conquers all, and chicks of a feather really should flock together. So maybe I'll see you in church on Sunday, or on some other day, at Chick-fil-A.

"I Love God!"

I don't remember how old the little boy was, but let's say ten or so. He came down the aisle at the pastor's invitation, and he said, "My name is Joey Kelly, and I love God." That was the most powerful statement I have ever heard.

My name is Bill Ivey, and I love God. Stop reading, not yet, but two paragraphs below, after I point out something and I say, "Now."

The same God Who so loved the world so much that He gave His only begotten Son that whosoever believeth on Him should not perish but have everlasting life - righteous almighty God - the One Who knew sin-debt payment on my behalf by Christ would be necessary - God knew that before He created man. Yet He created us anyway. He created us, even knowing of the crucifixion.

This might be a good time to pause and let Him tell you He loves you - you personally. Think about it. And tell Him you love Him. And let Him give you a nice big hug. "Now."

<3 <3 <3

When God became man and died on the cross, and rose again, He wasn't just accomplishing a goal. He was expressing enormous, infinite love. Yes, God made man for His glory. But He made man for His glory because He loved you. So in His love, you are His glory. Imagine that.

I am His glory. That is hard to grasp. But it is true. And He loves me. He wants to hug me. I am remembering Gracie Hart, played by Sandra Bullock in the movie *Miss Congeniality*, *singsonging*, "You think I'm gorgeous, you want to kiss me, you want to hug me, you want to love me."

When you are in Christ, you are gorgeous. But unlike the fun implication of Gracie's singsonging, Love is not self-seeking, we saw that in the Love Chapter of the Bible. Everything God wants to do for me, the hug he wants to give me, is to fill my need, not His, and He wants to do it because He loves me. Yes, my name is Bill Ivey and I love God.

No, it is not about me. It is about the One who created you and me. But it is also about *why* He created you and me.

<3 <3 <3

Visualize this. You have a child. Maybe you have a bunch of children, but just think about this one. This one needs you right now. This one loves you very much. This one child needs you so much. What do you want? You want only the best for this child. You want to spend time with this child. You want to give this child whatever he/she wants as long as it does not spoil him/her. You want to reassure this child you love him/her so so very very much. You spend time together - a lot of time together. The child's love grows. And grows.

Now picture God as the Father, and you as the adopted child. You learn that the Father sent His only *begotten* Son to die on the cross in your place, but His love for you didn't stop there. His love for you is here, right now, and it is so personal, and He wants so much for you to spend time with Him, and Know Love. He wants you to spend time with Him and know love that is perfect love. God is love, and He wants to share himself with you, through you, around you, in you, for you and forever.

Yes, God made us for His glory. We know, because the Bible tells us so, literally. But in my heart there rings a melody, there rings a melody of love, placed there by God, using the Bible in all its glory and the Holy Spirit with all His comfort. He could have done anything else and it would be glorious because whatever He does is glorious. God made us for His glory because He loved us, because God is love. God is perfect love through you, around you, in you, for you and forever.

Somehow, when you love someone, you want to tell them you love them. You want to show them you love them. God already told you,

Christ already showed you. Right now might be time for another hug.

God and you, His precious loved one, the one He wants to hug right now.

The one from whom He would so cherish right now hearing the words,

the words out loud, "I love you."

Just three little words, but oh how He loves that wonderful sound,

coming from you.

<3 <3 <3.

Chapter 17:

Secret Things and A Merry Heart

Remember, "If you want to make God laugh, tell him your plans?"
Well, for quite a few chapters now, I have been assuming that the chapter
I was finishing was the final chapter. I didn't check in with God about it, I
was just sure each was the final chapter. He hears my thoughts, so in that
sense I was telling Him my plans, and I didn't see any point in discussing
it with Him. I hope He likes to laugh, because I sure seem to make Him
do that a lot.

Of course, He doesn't need the benefit of "A merry heart does
good like medicine," for Him, but if I make Him laugh, I suspect He is
laughing with the knowledge that our sharing that laugh is doing me good
like medicine. And that might be a good positive form of bonding.

God works with each of us in a special way designed just for us.
Walk with God. He loves you, and wants to protect you. And sometimes,
He is the only one Who can. The only one Who will. The only one Who
can raise you up. The only one Who loves you enough to give you His all,
in His love, when the only thing that can help, is His all, in His love.
"With God nothing is impossible." It may take awhile. God is in the

details. It may take a long time. It may only take a day. But with God,

you have all the time in the world, and then some, if, you walk with God.

He yearns for you to walk with Him. He yearns for you. He yearns for

you! You can be as close to Him as you want to be, and, it is your move.

Secret Things:

In Chapter 9, I wrote regarding Lucifer's rebellion against God: "I

visualize, and this is just me visualizing it, I visualize that was followed

by all the evil in the universe swooping in, and being contained into one

body."

Remember that darkness is just an absence of light? Now I am

visualizing sort of the opposite of what I wrote. I am visualizing that

when the rebellion against God began, all the good (like light) went out of

Lucifer/Satan, and the resulting darkness, a complete lack of good (light)

left him with complete evil (darkness), and being completely evil, I mean

100% horrible, he would never, ever, allow the faintest sign of good

(light) back into him. Being complete evil, unlike passive darkness, he

actively would not and never will do such a thing as accept Jesus (the

truth, the light and the way) as his savior, nor will his demons. Since God

is love, and with God all things *all* things are possible, I wondered why

Satan would have to spend eternity suffering in hell. I think the answer is the choice was Satan's choice. He would never allow, much less invite, anything good into his heart. God has His rules, and for some reason(S) they are eternally important. They include righteousness. Thankfully that is righteousness with a throne of Grace. But if we, or demons, refuse to accept His grace, then we, or demons, in our free will choose eternal death. It is too late for Satan and demons. They made their choice, they *will* not to change, and their fate is sealed. They are so evil, they cannot undo it. They don't care. They just want to hate and to hurt anyone they can. But it is not too late for you, if you have even a glimmer of goodness in you. All it takes is a glimmer, and the Light of the World (Jesus) can do the rest. He stands at the door of your heart and knocks. Now is the time to invite Him in.

There is more I wonder about regarding those matters, yet I know God has omniscience beyond anything we can comprehend, and similarly, omnipotence. Being LOVE, whatever eternity brings, in His power and His omniscience and His Love, it is better than good. It is the good-est there could possibly be, because God is the good-est of good, the omniscient-est of omniscience, and the loving-est of love. Good wins. Slam dunk.

Brother Tom referred to "the secret things of God." God will reveal what He chooses to reveal when He chooses to reveal it. The history of Satan is of no consequence to us other than maybe it just puts some things in perspective. Maybe it answers some questions. But the focal point for now, and for eternity, is the Lord Jesus Christ, and what He did, and that He will reign for eternity, from a throne of grace with unlimited power, but from a throne of grace. I praise Him and thank Him that you and I can come in His love to that throne.

What we need to know more about is how to trust in Him now, and follow Him to stay away from evil and to draw nearer to Him and His love. Take time to bond with God. He wants to bond with you. Bonding generates trust. Really, bonding generates trust.

smile

SMILE, trusting

SMILE TRUSTING a merry heart

When your spirit is born again, your soul starts renewing and you can grow a MERRY HEART which does good, like medicine (liberally expanded paraphrase of Proverbs 17:22).

> You will show me the path of life;
> In Your presence *is* fullness of joy;
> At Your right hand *are* pleasures forevermore (Psalm 16:11).

When did you last associate God with "fullness of joy" and

"pleasures forevermore"? Did you know that if you know God, you know

love? Did you know that the surest way to know love is to give it away?

Did you know that knowing love, His love, and following Him with an

obedient heart, produces powerful medicine that is the best prescription

for reclaiming a merry heart? Did you know it was God who instigated

the joyous words, "Merry Christmas"? And who do you think coined the

gleeful term, "Happy Easter"?

> A merry heart does good, like medicine,
> But a broken spirit dries the bones.
> (Proverbs 17:22)

God and I know I am living proof that God can "un-break" a

broken spirit, give it a merry heart, and raise up "Dem bones, dem bones,

dem dry bones."

Having a merry heart IS like medicine. And the very best place to

have a merry heart is with God. That is not the only good place to have a

merry heart, but it is the very best place. In His infinite creative wisdom,

He created us such that loving Him is best for us, and loving Him with a

merry heart is priceless for our good health. Hey, He is not stupid. He

would not create us in such a way that the people who spend time with

Him would have better health if they were grouchy all day. Who wants Oscar the Grouch for his best buddy?

God makes my day. Just thinking about Abraham in God's presence, with Sarah eavesdropping at the door and laughing silently, with Abraham falling down on his face laughing. It makes me laugh, and makes my day.

You know, Abraham is known as the father of faith, and I always thought that faith was believing God exists. But Abraham was way past that. He knew God existed, and that is not faith. The Bible points out that believing the completely 100% obvious is not faith. Faith in God is believing things hoped for but unseen; believing them because God says they are true, and because you know the nature of God. Abraham absolutely knew God existed. So his faith was not faith in God's existence. His faith was in the fact that he trusted God, His goodness and His power, no matter what.

Isaac was precious to Abraham. Yet Abraham, surely knowing of God's love for him, trusted God enough to follow his instructions, regardless of the expected consequences. And at the other end of the spectrum, Abraham trusted God enough to feel comfortable falling down on his face laughing when God spoke. I stand amazed at Abraham's relationship with God. Sure, Abraham messed up, many times. So have we. But I so enjoy laughing when I think of that scene.

Has God ever made you laugh? Let Him make you laugh. Let Him tell you something almost impossible, like He told Abraham, that made Abraham fall down on his face laughing. Yes, the Throne of Grace is Holy ground, but your place near the Throne of Grace is also a playground your Father built just for you. A playground. Yes. A playground at the Throne of Grace. Just look above and read the words of Psalms 16:11 and Proverbs 17:22 again. Then notice how pretty are the numbers, and the *coincidental* progression, 16/17 and 11/22 is a thing of beauty, created by the Lord, for us to notice, like flowers in springtime at a playground of love. I realize non-CPA's may not grasp such beauty in numbers. Maybe they grasp other beauty. Beauty truly is in the eye of the beholder, and God made each eye in a way that it can see as beauty whatever God intended it to be able to see a beauty. And then He said, "Don't worship the creature rather than the Creator." So let's don't forget that.

You still don't think God has a tremendous creative sense of humor? Were you ever the first person to invent a giraffe? Even a zebra? A donkey that could talk (Numbers 22) and another one that could write a book? You don't believe about the playground at the Throne of Grace? About the donkey who could write? Impossible, you say? "With God all things are possible." Want proof? Here it is: I just wrote a book. In Love. With Him. For you.

IN MEMORIAM:

Thomas O. Norton

August 3, 1926 - July 10, 2010

Sound bites, Brother Tom:

"In all my years of going into the prisons,
I never met one prison inmate that God didn't love. Not one!"
"They don't care how much you know,
until they know how much you care."
"How can two walk together lest they be agreed?"
"Forget about the mule. Load the wagon."
"Information brings inspiration."
"I love you, brother."

Brother Tom 1996:

"Since 1986, when we founded Highways and Hedges Christian Ministries, Inc., my wife and I have been blessed to have personal contact with over 12,000 men and women in the prison systems of our nation who have come to trust Jesus Christ as One who loves them. Many of these people quit trusting anyone a long time ago, and it does our hearts good to see them come to realize there is Somebody they can trust."

By 2010 the number of salvation decisions recorded on Highways and Hedges' computer totaled over 45,000.

Now a Brother Tom guiding passage, paraphrasing from

Matthew's Gospel, Chapter 25, and we close with Jesus having the last

word.

>
> Lord, when did we see you hungry, and feed You, or thirsty and
> give You drink?
> When did we see You a stranger and invite You in, or naked and
> clothe You?
> When did we see You sick and in prison and come to You?
>
> And He will answer,
> 'To the extent that you did it to one of these brothers of Mine,
> even the least of them, you did it to Me.'

Before closing this part of *Know Love* I think it is absolutely

necessary to mention that Highways & Hedges Christian Ministries was

and is blessed to have so many faithful volunteers serving the Lord.

Brother Tom specified that Jack Camp, Jr. should take over leadership at

Brother Tom's Passing. Jack accepted the challenge and today volunteers

are still serving with Jack, including his wife. Names that come to my

mind from over the years are Randy Owenby and his wife, the Kimseys,

the Meyerholtzs, and on and on. I apologize for not mentioning so many

others who answered the Lord's call to the Great Commission with

Highways & Hedges. But He knows all of them intimately. Having served

under Brother Tom, they would all say, give the Lord all the praise and all

the glory. But one more who comes to mind immediately is George

Chafin. George was Brother Tom's "go to guy" for computer help, and it is because of George that the historical numbers shown above are available. And the Lord would say to each of those named or referred to above, "Well done, my good and faithful servant."

Chapter 18:

And That Is What Love Is – For

Frank Daniels said, April 4, 2010, "Life should be lived joyfully, and laughed at regularly." I ask, "Why?"

And I answer, sin and joy, like fear and love, go together like total darkness and total light - you can't have one with the other. That is a reason we need to confess our sin quickly, go in a different direction, have no fear, and *enjoy* the light, *in joy!*

"Life should be lived joyfully, and laughed at regularly." Why?

The fullness of God includes joy, and I was delighted to find that Ephesians 3:17-19 says:

> "...that Christ may dwell in your hearts through faith; that you, being rooted and grounded in love, may be able to comprehend with all the saints what *is* the width and length and depth and height - to **know** the **love** of Christ which passes knowledge; that you may be filled with all the fullness of God."

We have seen so much focus on the time leading up to Jesus' crucifixion, and rightfully so. But that is *history.* Now the rest of *"His story"*: He overcame death; He is risen; He overcame the world; He wants our bodies to be the Holy Temple of His Spirit - but He knows sin and joy don't mix, and He wants you to choose *joy!*

"Life should be lived joyfully, and laughed at regularly."

Why? Because He earned it - for you!

Remember I told you I had a dream, while I was asleep. And someone named Christopher said to me, "You had a problem." The word "had" is past tense. When I woke up I did still have a problem. I learned that for sure within twenty-four hours. But Christopher used the word "had," past tense. God sees the future, and in the present He speaks as in the future, speaking of the past which is yet to come. I "knew" my "problem" would be in the past in the future, and that was encouragement enough for me.

In Isaiah 53:5, the Old Testament, of course, Isaiah wrote,

> But He *was* wounded for our transgressions,
> *He was* bruised for our iniquities;
> The chastisement for our peace *was* upon Him,
> And by His stripes we are healed.

Isaiah, in the past, was writing about something that would happen in the future - as if it already had happened - Jesus' paying the price for our sins - and writing as if the result for Isaiah was in the then present. And with Christ, already accepted by Isaiah, even though Jesus had not even yet been "born" on earth, the result of Christ's sacrifice in the New Testament was properly claimed by Isaiah in the Old Testament!

God does work with each of us in a special way designed just for us. Walk with God. He loves you and wants to protect you. And sometimes, He is the only one who can. The only one who will. The only one who can raise you up. The only one who loves you enough to give you His all, His self spit on and crucified, in His love, when the only thing that can help - is His all, in His love. "With God nothing is impossible." It may take a while. God is in the details. It may take a long time. It may only take a day. But with God, you have all the time in the world, and then some, if, you walk with God. He yearns for you to walk with Him. He yearns for you. He yearns for you!

I am wondering if we adequately covered the part about why God created us and what is going on with all the stuff that happens to us in our lives. Could we go back and address some of that?

Okay, I understand. God created us for His glory, and anything He creates gives Him glory, but instead of doing something else for His glory, He created us for His glory - because He loved us.

Also, our spirit has a soul that is growing here on earth in a temporary body. And this is a learning process and a time for us to be serving others, both our fellow man, and God.

And the single most significant thing that is being grown through the process is - love. God is love. And He is growing love inside us, in our souls. How does He do that?

I have said life on earth is a song in the midst of spiritual warfare. I have said life on earth is a process for growing our spirit's soul. I have said what we are really growing is love. How does God do that? He does it in a myriad of ways.

After using the word myriad, I went to the dictionary and looked it up. Dictionary.com says: "of an indefinitely great number; innumerable: the myriad stars of a summer night."

Yes, it fits. God grows love in a myriad of ways - an indefinitely great number of ways.

Everything that causes you to care about someone other than yourself, everything that causes you to care about your good name, a good name that can be a beacon of a role model for others who need such a role model - those are things God uses to grow His love in you and in others.

Every sin you ever committed, all things work together for good to those who love the Lord, and that good includes God growing love in you. God takes the good, the bad and the ugly - and uses it all to grow love. Maybe the bad is fertilizer, the good is sunshine and the ugly is the dark clouds on a rainy day - but that fertilizer, sunshine and rain is put just where God knows for it to be put - to maximize our growth in love.

With the sin that caused Jesus to be crucified on the cross - God took that and used it for good. With every sin in your life, God takes that and uses it for good. Only God can do such a thing, and do it a "myriad" of times in a myriad of circumstances - and even use it to grow love.

When it is all over, when we Christians all get to heaven, we will be able to see - like after we graduated from school, the little things that seemed so important in school, were not so important - except they were important in God growing love - they were important in planting seeds for God's flowers to bloom in the springtime of our new life - when we get to heaven we will be able to better see, all the things that confuse us so much now and are such a struggle for us while God is growing us here on earth, we will better be able to see the beautiful flowers that sprang from those seeds.

We are not under the law. The law, like all of our problems, is used as a tutor - as we, Christians, are under the Spirit. All things are *legal* for us, as far as not going to hell, but many things are not

"convenient." That word, convenient, used in that sentence, and used in a

similar sentence in the Bible means that some things bring bad results,

and under the Spirit we do not want to bring bad things, so for the

purposes of God's love in us, they are not "convenient." So again, under

the Spirit we do not want to bring bad things. Obedience to God would

usually still require obeying the Ten Commandments, but not for getting

to heaven, and it would usually be that we obey the Holy Spirit Who

reminds us of a "myriad" of things to do, rather than just following the

Ten Commandments as a tutor. That would be in accordance with

Proverbs 3:6 and a "myriad" of other wonderful verses.

It is good to strive to be more like Jesus, but be careful, because

now we are to focus on our loving Jesus, because of what He did for us,

and because God first loved us. God wants us to obey Him. But when it is

so hard, and we feel we just cannot always every minute obey Him, His

focus is no longer on His children obeying Him. His focus, as our focus

should be, is on the love between us. And on us loving Him. And even

when we are weak, our focus needs to be on loving Him. And His focus is

on bringing us to focus on loving Him, because nothing better can befall us than loving Him. Did I mention that our focus should be on our love for the Lord?

When we focus on our performance, even on our performance in obeying Him, we can become like Pharisees in that to the extent that we succeed in many areas of obedience, we thereby open a window for pride in our success; and on the other hand, when we fail in obeying Him, we can become disheartened. God wants us to obey Him, because that is always good. But even more than that - even more important than obeying Him on other things, the foremost thing we are called to do is - focus on loving Him. Did I mention that our focus should be on love?

Have you noticed God offers us a win-win situation? If we love Him and are - or are not successful in other things - we win. We always have the winning formula - the gift of love. And what a gift it is. Praise Him for such a gift as that. Praise the gift of love. God is Love.

Loving God is a gift - not from us, but from Him - all we have to do is accept the gift of His love for us, Him first loving us, for us to love Him - *a win-win situation.*

But what is love - for? More than anything else, love is for giving and forgiving.

Epilogue: Where True Love Is, "Sarah" Will Be.

God is not willing that any should perish, but that all should come to a saving knowledge of the Lord Jesus Christ. The Bible makes that clear. However, having given all of us a free will, would He override someone's free will ability to reject Jesus, so He can save that person? No, I wouldn't think He would ever override anyone's free will regarding grace. But He could lead others, like you and me, to plant seeds for a remedy. We could plant seeds by *praying* that the person come to a saving knowledge of the Lord Jesus Christ, and if already saved, be drawn closer to the Lord. Could He lead you to do that? For strangers? Doesn't the Golden Rule *require* it?

God even *promises* to answer our prayers that are in His will. He surely came through when folks prayed for my mother to be saved.

Remember Jesus asking Peter three times about his love for Jesus? Seriously, what about Jesus' Golden Rule? How can we just ignore that it exists? Wouldn't we want strangers to pray for our salvation? And the Golden Rule, as famous as it is, is *only* a helper. Why is the Golden Rule only a helper? Because it brings us into action as a beautiful flower of the Principal Principle. Love.

Arlen Williams. I never heard of him before either. But I heard about this today from a speech by Trey Gowdy at Liberty University. This is as close as I can remember how to describe it. Plane crash, some passengers killed immediately, others subject to death in the icy waters. Helicopter came and Arlen Williams took the rope, but he gave it to another passenger, and that person was flown to safety. Same thing again. And again. And again. Finally, the helicopter came back one last time for Arlen, but he was dead, from fatigue in the cold water.

What would Jesus have done? What did Jesus do? Arlen did it for strangers. He gave his life for strangers. Practicing *Sarah* is so easy compared to what Arlen and Jesus did. You don't have to give your life; just some time and focus. Jesus already gave His life, all we have to do in practicing Sarah is to pray. Yes it would include praying for strangers. But Arlen did not take time to become big buddies with the folks who needed him. And most people will never know who Arlen is and what he did. And most people you pray for will never know you prayed for them. If you were in ice water and about to die, or lost and going to literal burning hell, and knew it, would you want strangers to pray for you? I sure would.

What Jesus did was to obey His Father, and be crucified to save you and me. "If that isn't love what could love truly be?" Let's begin practicing *Sarah*. Know love. Know God is love as you let it flow through

280

you. Let it flow through you. Love is for giving. Give a little time for *Sarah* focus and the Lord can do the rest. In love. With you.

Summary of the case for practicing Sarah:

Jesus said we ought always to pray. And He said a lot of other things that indirectly but clearly tell us to pray practicing *Sarah.* How about Matthew 5:44, where He said, "...pray for those who spitefully use you and persecute you." That requires even more *compassion-ability* than, "Pray for strangers." Further, He wasn't saying pray that they win the lottery or continue to persecute you. Practicing *Sarah* for them would fit the context perfectly. It would fit the mind of Christ. It would fit love for eternity.

We can practice Sarah with confidence that God will honor it because He is not willing that any should perish and because it fits the Golden Rule; and the Golden Rule fits obedience to Jesus. And furthermore, practicing *Sarah* reflects love required by His promotion of the second greatest commandment.

Now, to close, here is a kind of "bedtime story" skit, for fun, and to enhance the grasping of the points. I claim Matthew 18:3-4 as my invitation and my excuse to quote Jesus saying as follows:

...unless you are converted and become as little children, you will by no means enter the kingdom of heaven.

Golden Rule bedtime story:

"Do unto others as you would have them do unto you."

Whenever you think of it - immediately pray for each person that you see (or think of) - that he/she will be saved, and if already saved, that he/she will be drawn closer to the Lord. That is called Sarah. *Also, whenever you have any thought that Jesus would not want you to have, let that be a reminder to practice* Sarah *immediately.* Being on offense with the Principal Principle, carries the side benefit of a virtually impenetrable defense, because you are staying on offense.

"But Coach, I don't have a *history* of praying for strangers." And Jesus said, "Peter, do you love me more than these others love me?" Peter said, "Coach, you know everything. You know I love you." Well, from that day forward Peter spoke *Sarah* with true love.

And sure enough, thereby, lo and behold, myriad myriads of prospective little lambs and grown-up sheep lived happily in the ever after. The end. Amen. Selah.